Reconstruction Era
Reference Library
Cumulative Index

KENT STATE UNIVERSITY LIBRARY, KENT, OHIO

Reconstruction Era
Reference Library
Cumulative Index

Cumulates Indexes For:

Reconstruction Era: Almanac
Reconstruction Era: Biographies
Reconstruction Era: Primary Sources

Lawrence W. Baker,
Project Editor

U·X·L
An imprint of Thomson Gale,
a part of The Thomson Corporation

THOMSON
GALE

Detroit • New York • San Francisco • San Diego • New Haven, Conn. • Waterville, Maine • London • Munich

Reconstruction Era Reference Library Cumulative Index

Project Editor
Lawrence W. Baker

Permissions
Margaret Abendroth, Denise Buckley,
Margaret Chamberlain

Imaging and Multimedia
Lezlie Light, Mike Logusz, Dan Newell,
Christine O'Bryan, Denay Wilding,
Robyn Young

Product Design
Pamela A. E. Galbreath, Kate Scheible

Composition
Evi Seoud

Manufacturing
Rita Wimberley

LIBRARY OF CONGRESS CATALOGING-IN-PUBLICATION DATA

Reconstruction era reference library cumulative index / Lawrence W. Baker.
    p. cm.
"Cumulates indexes for: Reconstruction era: almanac; Reconstruction era: biographies; Reconstruction era: primary sources."
  ISBN 0-7876-9220-4 (pbk.)
  1. Howes, Kelly King. Reconstruction era—Indexes. 2. Matuz, Roger. Reconstruction era—Indexes. 3. Grumet, Bridget Hall. Reconstruction era—Indexes. 4. Reconstruction (U.S. history, 1865–1877)—Juvenile literature—Indexes. 5. Almanacs, American—Juvenile literature—Indexes. 6. Reconstruction (U.S. history, 1865–1877)—Biography—Juvenile literature—Indexes. 7. Reconstruction (U.S. history, 1865–1877)—Sources—Juvenile literature—Indexes. I. Baker, Lawrence W.

  E668.H86 2004 Index+
  016.9738—dc22

                                                                    2004017310

This title is also available as an e-book.
1-4144-0454-9
Contact your Thomson Gale sales representative for ordering information.

Printed in the United States of America
10 9 8 7 6 5 4 3 2 1

Reconstruction Era Reference Library Cumulative Index

A = Reconstruction Era: Almanac
B = Reconstruction Era: Biographies
PS = Reconstruction Era: Primary Sources

A

AAAS (American Association for the Advancement of Science) **B:** 163

Abolition. *See* Abolitionists

Abolitionists. *See also* Slavery
 A: 13–14
 African American suffrage and, **PS:** 165
 Anthony, Susan B., and, **B:** 11–12
 Douglass, Frederick, *A:* 22–23; **PS:** 48–49
 Fourteenth Amendment and, **PS:** 89–90
 Garrison, William Lloyd, *A:* 14, 14 (ill.)
 Howe, Julia Ward, and; **B:** 126, 127
 Johnson, Andrew, and, *A:* 35; **PS:** 69
 Lincoln, Abraham, and, **PS:** 68
 political rights for African Americans and, **PS:** 102
 Stevens, Thaddeus, and, **B:** 182

Sumner, Charles, *A:* 106–7; **B:** 189; **PS:** 114
 Ten Per Cent Plan and, *A:* 43
 Weekly Tribune and, **B:** 92
 women's rights and, **PS:** 94–95
 women's suffrage and, *A:* 113, 114

Abuse, of African Americans
 PS: 78

Academy of Natural Sciences of Philadelphia
 B: 111

Accommodationists
 A: 200–201

Accommodations, equal access to
 A: 150

Acculturation
 B: 121

Activism, African American
 A: 204, 206–7

Activists, women's rights. *See* Women's rights

Adams, Henry
 A: 186

Adams, John
 B: 137

Adams, John Quincy
B: 144
PS: 120
Advertisements, newspapers, for lost relatives
A: 59
PS: 25
African American churches
A: 60–61, 61 (ill.), 62–63
African American ministers
A: 61, 63
African American schools
A: 64, 65 (ill.)
churches and, **A:** 63
Freedmen's Bureau and, **A:** 87, 109
Southern United States and, **A:** 92
African American suffrage. *See also* Fifteenth Amendment; Fourteenth Amendment; Voting rights
A: 37, 38, 44, 71, 130–31
PS: 53–54
becoming reality, **A:** 117–18
debate and compromise on, **PS:** 71, 88–89, 91, 166, 168
Douglass, Frederick, and, **A:** 23; **PS:** 52, 98
effects of, **PS:** 135–36
in elections of 1867, **A:** 135
elections of 1868 and, **PS:** 168, 169
end of slavery and, **PS:** 165
Fourteenth Amendment and, **A:** 112–13
illiteracy and, **PS:** 106
Johnson, Andrew, and, **A:** 94; **PS:** 46, 106
Lincoln, Abraham, and, **A:** 48
racial riots and, **A:** 115
Radical Republicans and, **A:** 104, 108
Republican Party and, **A:** 105
Stephens, Alexander, on Georgia and, **PS:** 71–74
U.S. Congress and, **PS:** 94

African Americans. *See also* Free African Americans; Redemption movement; Slavery; specific African American politicians
activism of, **A:** 204, 206–7
bank for, **PS:** 44
Black Codes and, **A:** 91–94, 93 (ill.)
celebrate war's end, **A:** 47
citizenship responsibilities and, **A:** 118, 146
civil rights for, **PS:** 71, 72
Civil War and, **B:** 154–55; **PS:** 15, 16, 124 (ill.)
after Civil War, **PS:** 30–31, 31 (ill.), 34
cotton and, **A:** 33 (ill.), 40, 42 (ill.), 157 (ill.)
courts and, **A:** 70
demands of, **A:** 130
discussing politics, **PS:** 53 (ill.)
disenfranchisement of, **A:** 140–41, 160, 161, 162 (ill.), 176–78, 194–95, 199; **PS:** 46, 88 (ill.), 100 (ill.), 106, 156, 166, 170, 190, 192 (ill.), 203–5
education and, **A:** 1–2, 46 (ill.), 64–65, 65 (ill.), 69–70, 92, 149, 158; **B:** 18, 24; **PS:** 41, 134
educational institutions of, **A:** 87, 196–97, 200–201, 202, 204; **PS:** 43, 54 (ill.), 131
in elections of 1867, **A:** 135, 137
in elections of 1868, **A:** 137, 140–41, 160; **PS:** 64, 167–68
elections of 1876 and, **PS:** 196–97
Emancipation Proclamation of 1863 and, **A:** 30–31, 31 (ill.)
as employees on plantations, **PS:** 39
employment, **A:** 158
enfranchisement of, **PS:** 52, 53–54

equal rights for, **A:** 9, 14, 37; **PS:** 78, 79
Forrest, Nathan Bedford, and, **PS:** 161
Freedmen's Bureau and, **PS:** 39–40
Freedmen's Bureau school, **PS:** 42 (ill.)
Freedmen's Conventions and, **A:** 127–30
freedom's effects on, **A:** 56–65
in Georgia, **A:** 39 (ill.)
as governors, **PS:** 132
harvesting cotton, **PS:** 25 (ill.)
Howard, Oliver Otis, and, **A:** 69, 86–87
identity questions of, **A:** 131
illiteracy and, **PS:** 106, 123, 142
integration and, **A:** 5, 134, 150
Johnson, Andrew, and, **A:** 81–82, 94, 105, 109; **PS:** 43, 109
justice system and, **PS:** 43, 78–79, 186
Ku Klux Klan and, **PS:** 130, 135, 153, 155–56, 159 (ill.)
labor system and, **A:** 67, 68, 156–58
land and, **PS:** 19, 23–25, 31–32, 35–36, 38–39
landownership and, **A:** 45–47, 67–68, 83–85, 103, 119–20, 134–35, 150
in law enforcement, **A:** 152, 196; **PS:** 130
laws concerning, **PS:** 19, 47, 48, 49, 69–70, 77, 80–81, 85
in Liberia, **PS:** 18
Lincoln, Abraham, and, **A:** 48
migrations of, **A:** 56–57, 82–83, 197 (ill.), 197–98, 205; **PS:** 25, 26, 205
military service, **B:** 56–57

mistreatment of, *PS:* 31, 78

obstacles faced by, *A:* 127

options for freed slaves, *PS:* 26

political cartoon against, *PS:* 191 (ill.)

at political conventions, *A:* 133–34

political rights and, *A:* 37–38, 134, 170

in politics and government, *A:* 61, 63, 150–53; *PS:* 74, 105–6, 122–26, 130–32, 134–36, 137 (ill.), 138–41, 147, 149

population counts and, *PS:* 12, 70, 71

Populism and, *A:* 202–3

racial problems, *B:* 81

Reconstruction era and southern, *A:* 9

Redemption criminal code and, *A:* 195–96

as refugees, *PS:* 28 (ill.)

Republicans and, *PS:* 168, 169, 182

school children, *A:* 134 (ill.)

Sea Islands and, *A:* 39–40

as sharecroppers, *A:* 157–58, 195; *PS:* 22, 26

as slaves after freedom, *PS:* 22, 26, 27–29

as soldiers, *A:* 2, 20–25, 36, 37 (ill.); *PS:* 15, 20, 124 (ill.)

in Southern Reconstruction governments, *A:* 170–71, 193

store owners taking advantage of, *PS:* 65

strong Southern communities of, *A:* 196–97

taking leading roles in Reconstruction, *A:* 148

Union League and, *A:* 131, 132; *PS:* 127

Union troops providing for, *PS:* 34–35, 36

violence against, *PS:* 69, 78, 97–98, 99 (ill.), 101, 105–6, 153, 155–56, 159 (ill.)

violence against Southern, *A:* 58, 70, 89, 129, 140, 159, 160, 171, 181 (ill.)

violence committed by, *PS:* 155

voting for first time, *PS:* 105, 105 (ill.)

voting rights, *B:* 57, 81

vs. white Southern voters, *PS:* 105, 135

African Methodist Episcopal (AME) Church
B: 153, 154

Africans
A: 12, 13
PS: 18, 20

After the War: A Southern Tour (Reid)
PS: 24

Agassiz, Elizabeth
B: 71

Agassiz, Louis
B: 71, 163

Agnew Clinic (Eakins)
B: 67

Agnew, Spiro
PS: 119

Agriculture Department
B: 167

Ah Sin
B: 103, 104

Akerman, Amos T.
A: 162
PS: 162

Alabama
PS: 17, 102, 105
Selma to Montgomery march, *A:* 207 (ill.)

Alabama
B: 82

Alaska
PS: 120

Alaska Purchase
B: 143

Alcohol avoidance
PS: 205–6

Alcorn, James L.
A: 133
B: 19, 21

Alcorn University
A: 197
B: 153, 159, 160
PS: 131

Alcott, Amos Bronson
B: 1–2

Alcott, Louisa May
B: 1 (ill.), **1–8**

AMA (American Missionary Association)
B: 25–26

AME (African Methodist Episcopal) Church
B: 153, 154

American Academy of Arts and Letters
B: 124, 131

American Academy of Political and Social Science
B: 24–25

American Anti-Slavery Society
PS: 165, 169

American Association for the Advancement of Science (AAAS)
B: 163

American Association of University Women
B: 166

American Civil War. *See also* Confederacy
A: 1, 4–5, 27–49
African American regiments in, *PS:* 55
African American school children during, *A:* 134 (ill.)
African Americans after, *PS:* 30–31, 31 (ill.), 34
African Americans and, *B:* 154–55; *PS:* 15, 16, 20, 124 (ill.)
Alcott, Louisa May, and, *B:* 3–4
baseball and, *B:* 220
beginning, *A:* 16–18; *B:* 78, 172
Cooke, Jay, and, *B:* 44
devastating toll of, *PS:* 2–3, 5, 9
Eakins, Thomas, and, *B:* 63
end of, *B:* 36, 80, 214; *PS:* 1
financing, *B:* 46–48
Fish, Hamilton, and, *B:* 84

Grant, Ulysses S., and, *A:* 138–39; *B:* 78–80

Great Britain and, *B:* 82–83, 85

Greeley, Horace, and, *B:* 93–94

Hampton, Wade, in, *A:* 184

Hayden, Ferdinand V., and, *B:* 107

Hayes, Rutherford B., in, *A:* 182; *B:* 115; *PS:* 197

Howard, Oliver Otis, and, *A:* 86

Howe, Julia Ward, and, *B:* 127

Howe, Samuel Gridley, and, *B:* 127

Johnson, Andrew, during, *PS:* 108, 113

Lee, Robert E., and, *B:* 34, 35–36

Lincoln, Abraham, and, *A:* 2, 4, 5, 7; *PS:* 12, 13

Native Americans and, *B:* 148–49

newly freed slaves during, *PS:* 14 (ill.)

Radical Republicans and, *A:* 108

Revels, Hiram, and, *B:* 154–55

Schurz, Carl, and, *A:* 90

slavery and, *A:* 4–5, 17, 18–20, 30, 51

slaves picking cotton during, *PS:* 60 (ill.)

Smalls, Robert, in, *A:* 154

Stephens, Alexander, and, *B:* 37–38

Stevens, Thaddeus, and, *A:* 102; *B:* 183–84

Sumner, Charles, and, *A:* 107

Tilden, Samuel J., and, *B:* 201–2

Toombs, Robert A., and, *B:* 40

Vance, Zebulon, and, *B:* 212–14

women's roles and, *PS:* 60–61

The American Conflict (Greeley)
B: 94

American Fur Company
B: 106

American Home Economics Association
B: 167

American Indians. *See* Native Americans

American Jurist
B: 190

American Missionary Association (AMA)
B: 25–26

American Party
B: 210

American Revolution
B: 210

American Watercolor Society
B: 75

American West expedition
B: 106–11, 109 (ill.), 111 (ill.)

American Woman Suffrage Association (AWSA)
B: 12–13, 15, 124, 129

Americo-Liberians
PS: 18

Ames, Adelbert
A: 152, 177–78, 178 (ill.)
B: 18, 155, 159

Ames, Mary
A: 1–2

Ames, Oakes
PS: 175–76, 177–78, 178 (ill.), 179–80, 180 (ill.), 181

Amicus, Jacksonis. *See* Tilden, Samuel J.

Amnesty. *See also* Pardons
A: 74, 80, 88, 168

Anderson, Jourdon
A: 54–55
PS: 32

Anderson, P. H.
PS: 32

Andrews, Sidney
PS: 40, 64

Annexation treaty
B: 83, 84

Anthony, Captain
B: 53

Anthony, Susan B.
A: 111 (ill.), 114
B: 9 (ill.), **9–16**, 14 (ill.), 129, 131
PS: 95

Antietam, Battle of
PS: 9

Anti-immigration bill, Chinese and
B: 19, 120, 121 (ill.)

Anti-Masonic Party
B: 182

Antislavery movement. *See* Abolitionists

Antislavery newspapers
A: 14, 15 (ill.)
PS: 49

Antiwar protests
A: 20

Appleton's Journal
B: 69, 71–72, 73

Arapaho
B: 150, 151

"Argument for the Impeachment of President Johnson" (Sumner). *See also* Articles of Impeachment; Impeachment, of Johnson, Andrew
PS: **108–21**

Aristocracy, plantation
A: 12, 85–88

Arkansas
A: 152, 160
First Reconstruction Act of 1867 and, *PS:* 102
Ku Klux Klan in, *PS:* 156
Lincoln, Abraham, Reconstruction plan and, *PS:* 68

Armstrong, Samuel Chapman
A: 200

"Appeal to Womanhood throughout the World" (Howe)
B: 130

Art Journal
B: 73

Arthur, Chester A.
B: 21

Articles of Impeachment. *See also* "Argument for the Impeachment of President Johnson" (Sumner); Impeachment, of Johnson, Andrew
B: 141
Ashley, James M.
A: 104
Assassination, of Lincoln, Abraham
B: 33, 174, 175
PS: 68
Association for the Advancement of Women
B: 163
Association of Collegiate Alumnae. *See* American Association of University Women
Astor, Emily
B: 125
Astronomy
B: 163
Atlanta Compromise
A: 200, 204
Atlantic Monthly
B: 58, 100, 101–2, 127
PS: 49
Auld, Hugh
B: 53
Auld, Sophia
B: 53
Auld, Thomas
B: 53, 55
Aunt Jo's Scrap-Bag (Alcott)
B: 7
Authors. *See* Writers
Avery, Charles
B: 26
Avery Institute
B: 23, 26
AWSA. *See* American Woman Suffrage Association (AWSA)

B

Babcock, Orville E.
B: 84–85, 86–87
PS: 181, 182

Badlands of Dakota territory
B: 106–7
Báez, Bonaventura
B: 83, 85
Ballot box-stuffing
PS: 196, 206
Ballots, punch card
PS: 197
Bank, Freedman's Savings
PS: 44
Bankers
B: 44–51
Banking syndicates
B: 49
Banknotes
B: 45
Bankruptcy
Anthony, Susan B., and, *B:* 13
Cooke, Jay, and, *B:* 44, 50
Grant, Ulysses S., and, *B:* 87
Banks, Nathaniel B.
A: 37, 41
PS: 35
Barnard, A. M. *See* Alcott, Louisa May
Barnburners
B: 201
Baseball
first professional team, *B:* 221, 223–24
invention of, *B:* 220–21
professional leagues, *B:* 218, 220, 223–24
Wright, Harry, *B:* 218, 219 (ill.), 219–25
Baseball (Eakins)
B: 66
Baseball Hall of Fame. *See* National Baseball Hall of Fame
Bates, Edward
B: 48
"The Battle Hymn of the Republic" (Howe)
B: 124, 127–28
Battle of Antietam (1862)
PS: 9
Battle of Brice's Crossroads (1864)
PS: 160

Battle of Little Big Horn (1876)
B: 87, 120, 151
Battle of the Bloody Angle (1864–65)
B: 80
Behind the Scenes in Washington (Martin)
PS: 173–84
Belknap, William W.
B: 87
PS: 174
Bell, John
B: 211 (ill.), 212
Bethlehem to Jerusalem
B: 74
Beyond the Mississippi (Richardson)
B: 71
Bingham, John A.
A: 105
B: 142 (ill.)
PS: 90–91, 113 (ill.)
Birchard, Sardis
B: 113, 114, 116
The Birth of a Nation (Griffith)
A: 208, 208 (ill.)
Black Codes
A: 68, 74, 91–94, 93 (ill.), 100, 195
B: 76, 196
PS: 19, 47, 49, 69–70, 77–78, 80–81
Civil Rights Bill and, *A:* 109–10
labor source and, *PS:* 85
Reconstruction governments and, *A:* 149
U.S. Congress and, *PS:* 87, 91
Black Friday
B: 82
PS: 174
Black Hawk War
B: 32
Black Panthers
A: 206
Black Reconstruction in America (Du Bois)
PS: 140–41
Blacks. *See* African Americans

Blaine, James G.
 A: 105
 B: 116
Blair, Francis P., Jr.
 A: 137 (ill.), 140 (ill.)
 PS: 167 (ill.), 168
Blair, Francis P., Sr.
 PS: 80
Blair, Norvel
 PS: 31
Bland-Allison Act of 1878
 B: 120
Bliss, Amos
 B: 90
Bloomer, Amelia
 B: 11
Bonds
 B: 46–48
Bonnat, Léon
 B: 64
Booth, John Wilkes
 A: 48
 B: 174
Border states. *See also* specif-
  ic border states
 A: 2
 PS: 14, 17
"Boss" Tweed. *See* Tweed,
  William Marcy "Boss"
Boston Christian Register
 B: 100
Boston Red Stockings
 B: 223, 224
Bouchet, Edward
 B: 24–25
Boutwell, George S.
 B: 142 (ill.)
Bowers, Claude G.
 A: 208
Boycotts, Montgomery bus
 A: 206
Boyer, Benjamin M.
 PS: 166
Bozeman Trail
 B: 148, 149
Bradley, Joseph P.
 B: 118
 PS: 191–92
Brains. *See* Sweeny, Peter Barr
Brazil
 PS: 3, 20
Bribes
 PS: 145, 174, 175

Brice's Crossroads, Battle of
 PS: 160
Bridgman, Laura
 B: 125
Bristow, Benjamin H.
 B: 86
British Honduras, former
  Confederates in
 PS: 3
Broderick, Matthew
 PS: 55
Brooklyn Atlantics
 B: 224
Brooks, James
 PS: 178 (ill.)
Brooks, Preston
 A: 106
 B: 193 (ill.), 194
 PS: 120
Brown, George T.
 PS: 111 (ill.)
Brown, John
 B: 35, 56
Brown, Joseph E.
 B: 37
Brown v. Board of Education
 A: 199, 206
 PS: 193
Bruce, Blanche K.
 A: 151, 151 (ill.)
 B: 17 (ill.), **17–22**
 PS: 131
Brulé Sioux
 B: 147, 148
Brunell, Mary
 PS: 18
Bryant, William Cullen
 B: 74
Buchanan, James
 B: 170, 172, 197
Bull Bear
 B: 147
Bullock, Rufus B.
 PS: **144–52**, 146 (ill.)
Bunche, Ralph
 A: 207 (ill.)
Bureau of Indian Affairs
 B: 87, 120–21
Bureau of Refugees, Freed-
  men, and Abandoned
  Lands. *See* Freedmen's
  Bureau

Burning crosses
 PS: 163–64
Bus segregation
 A: 206
Bush, George W.
 PS: 197
Butler, Andrew
 B: 194
 PS: 120
Butler, Benjamin F.
 A: 17–18, 36
 B: 142 (ill.)
Butler, David
 B: 81
Butler, Pierce
 PS: 58, 65, 66
Butterflies
 B: 109

C

California
  Fourteenth Amendment
    and, *PS:* 96
  land claims, *B:* 170
Cameron, Simon
 B: 172, 172 (ill.)
Campbell, John
 A: 161 (ill.)
Campbell, Tunis G.
 A: 128
Canal Ring
 B: 204
Canals, Central America and
 B: 121–22
The Capture of Jefferson Davis
  (Harnden)
 PS: 8
Cardozo, Francis L.
 A: 128
 B: 23 (ill.), **23–29**
Cardozo, W. Warrick
 B: 25
Caribbean, African slaves in
 PS: 20
Carmany, John H.
 B: 101
Carnegie, Andrew
 A: 200
Carpet-Bag Rule in Florida
  (Wallace)
 PS: 196–97

Carpetbaggers
   A: 8–9, 133, 147–48,
      170–71, 192–93
   B: 19, 41
   PS: 144–46, 151, 153, 198
Cartoons, editorial. *See* Polit-
   ical cartoons
Cartwright, Alexander
   B: 220, 221 (ill.)
Cass, Lewis
   B: 191
Casserly, Eugene
   B: 158
Censure, of Ames, Oakes
   PS: 181
Centennial Exposition
   B: 64, 66, 73
Central America
   B: 121–22
Century
   B: 87
Century Building and Loan
   Association
   B: 25
Chalmers, H. H.
   PS: 136
Chamberlain, Daniel H.
   A: 184, 185
   PS: 140, 195, 199
Chandler, Zachariah
   A: 77, 80
Channing, William Ellery
   B: 190
Charleston, South Carolina
   PS: 57
Chase, Salmon P.
   B: 46, 47, 47 (ill.), 48, 137
Chemistry, industrial
   B: 165
*The Chemistry of Cooking and
   Cleaning* (Richards)
   B: 165
Chemists
   B: 161–67, 165 (ill.)
Cheney, Mary Youngs. *See*
   Greeley, Mary
Chess Players (Eakins)
   B: 66
Chevalier of the Order of St.
   Savior
   B: 126
Cheyenne (Native Americans)
   B: 148, 149, 150, 151

Chicago World's Fair
   B: 166
Chief Joseph
   B: 87
Chief Smoke
   B: 147
Children's literature
   B: 4–5
China, treaties with
   B: 120
Chinese, disenfranchise-
   ment of
   PS: 168
Chinese immigrants
   A: 163
   B: 19, 120, 121 (ill.)
Chivington, John H.
   B: 149
Churches
   A: 60–61, 61 (ill.), 62–63
Cincinnati Commercial
   A: 54
Cincinnati Red Stockings
   B: 218, 221, 222 (ill.),
      223–24, 225
Cities
   blacks in, *A:* 56–57, 82–83,
      158, 205; *PS:* 25, 26
   in ruins, *PS:* 2 (ill.), 3, 28
      (ill.), 57
Citizenship. *See also* Civil
   Rights Act of 1866;
   Fourteenth Amend-
   ment
   A: 118, 146
   B: 57
Civil rights
   PS: 71, 72, 88, 91, 92
   Blanche, Bruce K., and, *B:*
      19–20
   Creoles, *A:* 37
   Douglass, Frederick, and,
      A: 22–23; *B:* 56, 57
   Grant, Ulysses S., and, *B:*
      76
   Johnson, Andrew, and, *A:*
      71, 77, 110; *B:* 138
   Reconstruction era and,
      A: 9, 70–71, 134
   Republicans and, *A:* 105,
      110, 111
   Sumner, Charles, and, *B:*
      196, 197

Civil Rights Act of 1866
   PS: 48, 49, 78, 85, 188
   Fourteenth Amendment
      and, *PS:* 88, 91
   Johnson, Andrew, and,
      PS: 79–84, 116
   Rogers, Andrew J., on, *PS:*
      90
   U.S. Congress and, *PS:* 87,
      91
   veto by Johnson, Andrew,
      77–86
Civil Rights Act of 1875
   A: 168, 180
   B: 81
   PS: 85, 185–91, 205
Civil Rights Act of 1964
   A: 113, 206
Civil Rights Bill
   A: 109–10, 110 (ill.), 111
Civil rights movement
   A: 190, 205, 206–7
Civil service
   A: 173
Civil service reform
   B: 118–19
Civil War. *See* American
   Civil War
Cleveland, Grover
   B: 138
Clinton, Bill
   PS: 112
Coins, vs. paper currency
   B: 45
Colfax, Schuyler
   A: 137 (ill.)
   B: 83, 158
   PS: 79, 167 (ill.), 175 (ill.),
      175–76, 177–81, 181
      (ill.)
Colleges and universities.
   See also specific colleges
   and universities
   African American, *A:* 87,
      196–97, 200–201, 202,
      204; *PS:* 43, 131
   Anthony, Susan B., and,
      B: 15
   for women, *B:* 163
Colonialism
   A: 203
Colored Preparatory High
   School. *See* Paul Lau-

rence Dunbar High
School
Colored Tennessean
   A: 59
The Commonwealth
   B: 126
Communal living, Alcott,
   Louisa May, and
   B: 2
Communism
   A: 203
Communist Party USA
   (CPUSA)
   A: 203
*A Compendium of the History
   of the United States*
   (Stephens)
   B: 38
**"A Complete and Graphic
   Account of the Crédit
   Mobilier Investiga-
   tion"** (Martin)
   PS: 173–84
*A Comprehensive and Popular
   History of the United
   States* (Stephens)
   B: 38
Compromise of 1850
   B: 56, 183, 192
Compromise of 1877
   A: 168, 183, 185–86
   B: 207
   PS: 198, 201
*Condensed Novels, and Other
   Papers* (Harte)
   B: 100
Confederacy. *See also* South-
   ern United States
   PS: 13, 89, 93
   African American soldiers
   and, *A:* 25
   amnesty and, *A:* 80, 88
   Davis, Jefferson, and, *B:*
   31, 33
   debt, *PS:* 89, 93
   formation of, *A:* 7, 16
   Fourteenth Amendment
   and, *A:* 113–14; *B:*
   214–15
   Grant, Ulysses S., and, *B:* 78
   Johnson, Andrew, and, *A:*
   77, 80, 88–89

landownership and, *A:*
   83–84
   pardons and, *A:* 88–89
   Stephens, Alexander, and,
   B: 37
   Lee, Robert E., and surren-
   der of, *B:* 36, 80, 174
   Tennessee and, *A:* 78–79;
   B: 136
   Toombs, Robert A., and,
   B: 39, 40
   Vance, Zebulon, and, *B:*
   209, 213–14
Confederate Congress, slave
   soldiers and
   PS: 20
Confederate leaders. *See
   also* Davis, Jefferson;
   Lee, Robert E.;
   Stephens, Alexander;
   Toombs, Robert A.
   B: 30 (ill.), **30–43,** 32 (ill.),
   35 (ill.), 37 (ill.), 40 (ill.)
Confederate troops
   despair of, *PS:* 5–6
   end of the Civil War, *PS:*
   1, 3–4, 7
   evacuation and destruc-
   tion by, *PS:* 3, 5
   resentment of, *PS:* 7
   slave soldiers, *PS:* 20
Congress. *See* U.S. Congress
Congressional seats
   population counts and,
   PS: 12, 70
   "three-fifths compromise"
   and, *PS:* 12, 70
   voting rights and, *PS:* 89,
   91, 166–67
Conkling, Roscoe
   B: 19, 20 (ill.), 21
Connecticut, African American suffrage in
   PS: 89, 166
Connolly, Richard B.
   B: 203
Conquering Bear
   B: 148
Constitutional amendments.
   See also specific amend-
   ments
   A: 209

Constitutional Union Party
   B: 37, 40, 211 (ill.), 212
*A Constitutional View of the
   Late War Between the
   States* (Stephens)
   B: 38
Constitutionalist
   B: 90
Contraband
   A: 28, 32
Contracts. *See* Labor con-
   tracts
Convict lease system
   A: 196
Cooke, Jay
   A: 175–76
   B: 44 (ill.), **44–51,** 83, 107
Cooke's Castle
   B: 48
Cooper, James Fenimore
   B: 100
Cope, Alfred
   B: 24
Corbin, Abel Rathbone
   B: 82
   PS: 174
Correspondence schools
   B: 166
Corruption. *See also* Scan-
   dals
   African American politi-
   cians and, *PS:* 123–24
   Bullock, Rufus B., and, *PS:*
   150
   carpetbaggers and, *PS:*
   145, 151
   in Freedmen's Bureau, *PS:*
   40
   Grant, Ulysses S., and, *A:*
   163–64, 179 (ill.)
   Mississippi politicians
   and, *PS:* 124
   railroad companies and,
   PS: 175–80
   in Reconstruction govern-
   ments, *A:* 153–56, 171,
   192–93
   as sign of times, *PS:* 174
   South Carolina's African
   American legislators
   and, *PS:* 136, 140
   Tweed, William Marcy
   "Boss," and, *PS:* 174

U.S. Congress and, *PS:*
174
Cotton
PS: 25 (ill.), 60 (ill.)
African Americans and, *A:*
33 (ill.), 40, 42 (ill.),
157 (ill.)
Northerners and, *A:*
94–95
overproduction of, *A:* 156
Cotton States and International Exposition (1895)
A: 200
Coulter, E. Merton
PS: 127
Council of Congregationalist Ministers of Massachusetts
PS: 94
Courts
African Americans in, *PS:*
43, 78–79, 186
Freedmen's Bureau and,
A: 70
white terrorists and, *A:*
160
Cox, Jacob
PS: 80
CPUSA (Communist Party
USA)
A: 203
Crédit Mobilier scandal
B: 83
PS: 175–80, 181 (ill.)
Creoles
A: 36, 37
Cricket
B: 219
"The Crimes against Kansas"
speech (Sumner)
B: 193–94
Criminal code, of Redemption government
A: 195–96
Criminal defense
B: 170
Criminal trials, presidential
testimony in
PS: 182
The Crisis
A: 203
Crook, William H.
B: 173

Crosby, Peter
A: 177
Crosses, burning
PS: 163–64
CSA. *See* Confederacy
Cuba
B: 85
Cumberland Gap
B: 73 (ill.)
Currency
Anthony, Susan B., and,
B: 9
paper, *B:* 45
soft money and, *B:* 120
Current, Richard Nelson
PS: 151
Custer, George Armstrong
B: 87, 120, 150–51
Custer's Last Stand. *See* Battle of Little Big Horn

D

D. Appleton and Company
B: 71, 73
Daily Whig
B: 91
Dalziel Brothers
B: 70
Daughters of Temperance
B: 11
Davis Bend, Mississippi
A: 28, 41–42
Davis, David
B: 118
Davis, Henry Winter
A: 44
Davis, Jefferson
A: 16, 28, 41, 88
B: 30 (ill.), **30–34**, 32 (ill.),
195
PS: 8, 9–10, 131
Greeley, Horace, and, *B:*
33, 94
Revels, Hiram, and, *B:*
153, 156 (ill.)
Stanton, Edwin, and, *B:*
175
Davis, Joseph
A: 41, 42
Dawes Act
B: 151

Dawes, Henry L.
PS: 84
Debt
PS: 89, 93, 140–41, 151
Declaration of Independence
A: 13
Declaration of Rights of the
Women of the United
States
B: 13
Declaration of Sentiments
A: 112
B: 12
Declaration of Women's
Rights
B: 11, 56
Delano, Columbus
B: 110
Delany, Martin R.
A: 128
DeLarge, Robert
PS: 123
Delaware
A: 2, 16, 34
Emancipation Proclamation and, *PS:* 14
Fourteenth Amendment
and, *PS:* 96
Lincoln, Abraham, and,
PS: 19–20
Thirteenth Amendment
and, *PS:* 17
Democratic Party. *See also*
Southern Democrats
A: 15–16, 101
on African American suffrage, *PS:* 166
in elections of 1866, *A:*
117
in elections of 1867, *A:*
135
in elections of 1868, *A:*
137
in elections of 1874, *A:*
178–80; *PS:* 190
Greeley, Horace, and, *B:*
96
impeachment of Johnson,
Andrew, and, *PS:* 118
Ku Klux Klan and, *PS:* 156
national conventions, *B:*
96, 204

Radical Republicans and,
    A: 105, 108, 146
vs. Republicans, ***B:***
    116–18, 204, 206–7
Revels, Hiram, and, ***B:***
    159–60
slavery and, ***B:*** 201, 210
the South and, ***B:*** 119
Toombs, Robert A., and,
    B: 40
Dent, Frederick Tracy
    B: 77
Dent, Julia
    B: 77
Department of Agriculture
    B: 167
Department of Defense
    B: 172
Department of Defense,
    Freedmen's Bureau Act
    and
    PS: 36, 37
Department of Justice
    PS: 162, 163
Department of the Interior
    B: 108
Department of the Treasury
    B: 21, 48
Devil's Ford (Harte), gold
    mining camp from
    B: 101 (ill.)
DeYoung, John
    A: 69
The Dial
    B: 125
Dickens, Charles
    B: 100, 126
Dime novels
    B: 70–71
Dinosaur fossils
    B: 105, 107
Discrimination. *See also* Vot-
    ing rights
    PS: 85, 185–90
Disenfranchisement. *See*
    Voting rights
District of Columbia, African
    American suffrage in
    A: 117
Dodge, Greenville M.
    PS: 173
Doubleday, Abner
    B: 220

Douglas, Stephen
    A: 6
Douglass, Charles
    PS: 55
Douglass, Frederick
    A: 14, 19, 22–23, 23 (ill.),
        97–98, 151 (ill.)
    B: 10, 52 (ill.), **52–61**, 55
        (ill.), 57 (ill.)
    PS: 48 (ill.)
    as abolitionist, *PS:* 48–49
    on African American mi-
        gration, *A:* 197–98
    African American soldiers
        and, *A:* 21, 24
    on African American suf-
        frage, *PS:* 98
    on end of slavery, *PS:* 165
    equality and, *PS:* 49–52
    Fifteenth Amendment
        and, *PS:* 54
    on Fourteenth Amend-
        ment compromise, *PS:*
        89
    interracial marriage, *PS:* 55
    Johnson, Andrew, and, *A:*
        94
    "Reconstruction" by, *PS:*
        46–56, 49–52
    on Reconstruction era
        South, *PS:* 98
    women's suffrage and, *PS:*
        95
Douglass, Lewis
    PS: 55
Drake, Charles Daniel
    B: 158
Dred Scott decision (1857)
    PS: 79
Drew, George Franklin
    PS: 196
Du Bois, W. E. B.
    A: 149, 202–3, 203 (ill.),
        204, 204 (ill.)
    PS: 35, 41, 140–41
    on post-Reconstruction
        period, *A:* 198
    vs. Washington, Booker
        T., *A:* 201
Dubuclet, Antoine
    A: 36
Dunn, Oscar J.
    PS: 40

Dunning, William A.
    A: 208
The Duties of Defeat (Vance)
    B: 213

E

E. W. Clark & Company
    B: 45
Eager, Washington
    A: 160
Eakins, Benjamin
    B: 62–63
Eakins, Thomas
    B: 62 (ill.), **62–69,** 65 (ill.)
East Baltimore Mental Im-
    provement Society
    B: 53
Eastern Lakota
    B: 147, 148
Eastman, George
    A: 200
Eaton, John
    PS: 34–35
Ecology
    B: 165
Economic independence, for
    African Americans
    PS: 19
Economy. *See also* Financial
    crises
    B: 81–82, 120
    based on slave labor, *A:*
        12–13
    in Northern United States,
        A: 4, 162–63
    in Reconstruction era
        South, *A:* 66–67, 104,
        156, 171, 174, 176, 196
    in Southern United States,
        A: 4, 13; *PS:* 89, 93,
        140–41, 151
Edisto Island
    A: 1
Editorial cartoons. *See* Politi-
    cal cartoons
Education
    African American institu-
        tions, *A:* 158, 196–97,
        200–201, 202, 204; *PS:*
        41, 42 (ill.), 43, 54 (ill.),
        131

African Americans and, *A:*
1–2, 3, 46 (ill.), 64–65,
65 (ill.), 69–70, 92, 149,
158; *B:* 18, 24; *PS:* 41
Alcott, Amos Bronson,
and, *B:* 1–2
Blanche, Bruce K., and, *B:*
18
Bouchet, Edward, and, *B:*
24–25
Cardozo, Francis L., and,
B: 23, 25–26
former slaves and, *PS:* 134
Hayes, Rutherford B., on,
PS: 203
home economics in, *B:*
166, 167
integration in, *A:* 134,
150; *PS:* 193
in Reconstruction era
South, *A:* 149
in Redemption govern-
ment, *A:* 194
Stevens, Thaddeus, and,
B: 182
vocational, *A:* 200–201,
204
women and, *B:* 163, 164,
166
Eggleston, George Cary
PS: 4
Eight Cousins (Alcott)
B: 6
Eighteenth Amendment
PS: 206
Elected offices
African Americans in, *PS:*
74, 122, 125, 130–31,
135
former Confederates and,
PS: 89, 92–93, 98,
148–49, 155
Elections
of 1865, *A:* 88
of 1866, *A:* 117
of 1867, *A:* 135, 137
of 1868, *A:* 137 (ill.),
137–41, 140 (ill.), 160;
PS: 64, 167 (ill.),
167–68, 173
of 1870, *PS:* 156
of 1872, *PS:* 169, 181; *A:*
162, 174

of 1874, *A:* 177–80; *PS:*
190
of 1876, *A:* 180 (ill.),
180–85; *B:* 116–18, 117
(ill.), 119, 199, 204, 205
(ill.), 206 (ill.), 206–7;
PS: 195–98, 201, 204
(ill.)
of 1878, *PS:* 206
of 2000, *PS:* 197
African American voters
in, *A:* 146
buying votes in, *PS:* 174
Enforcement Acts and, *A:*
160–62
fraud in, *A:* 183; *PS:*
196–97, 206
in Reconstruction era
South, *PS:* 105, 135
violence and intimidation
in, *A:* 140–41, 160, 162
(ill.), 176–78, 194–95;
PS: 105–6, 156, 190,
192 (ill.)
Electoral College
B: 118
Electoral commission
B: 117–18, 207
Elegant Oakey. *See* Hall, A.
Oakey
Elliott, Robert Brown
PS: 122–23, 124 (ill.)
Emancipation. *See also* Free-
dom; Thirteenth
Amendment
A: 18–20, 19 (ill.)
PS: 3, 14–15, 202
American Civil War and,
A: 30–31
rejoicing over, *A:* 31 (ill.),
52–54, 189–90
Emancipation Proclamation
of 1863
A: 7, 18–20, 30–31, 51,
204–5
B: 18, 56, 155
PS: 13 (ill.), 14, 15
Emerson, Ellen
B: 2
Emerson, Lidian
B: 2
Emerson, Ralph Waldo
B: 2, 125, 190

Enforcement Act of 1870
A: 139, 144, 160–62, 175
B: 81
Enfranchisement. *See* Voting
rights
Engraving, wood
B: 70
Environmental chemistry
B: 165
Equal Pay Act of 1963
A: 113
Equal rights. *See also* specific
civil rights acts
African Americans in
courts and, *PS:* 43,
78–79
after American Civil War,
PS: 185
Douglass, Frederick, and,
PS: 49–52
Hayes, Rutherford B., and,
PS: 198, 199, 201, 202
Johnson, Andrew, and,
PS: 81, 82, 113–14
Pike, James Shepherd,
and, *PS:* 136
readmission to Union
and, *PS:* 67, 101
Sumner, Charles, pushes
for, *PS:* 185–87
Equality
A: 4, 9, 71
Creoles and, *A:* 37
disagreement over, *A:* 14
Fourteenth Amendment
and, *A:* 114–15
Radical Republicans and,
A: 105, 108, 126
Etheridge, Emerson
A: 93–94
European immigrant disen-
franchisement
PS: 168
Everett, Edward
B: 211 (ill.)
Every Saturday
B: 101–2
Exoduster movement
A: 190, 197 (ill.), 197–98
Expeditions
B: 106–11, 109 (ill.), 111
(ill.)

F

Fairfield, Flora. *See* Alcott, Louisa May

Family and consumer sciences. *See* Home economics

Family reunions
  A: 59–60

Family, searching for
  PS: 25–26, 29–30

Farrar, Charles A.
  B: 162

Federal office, Fourteenth Amendment and
  B: 214–15

Feminist leaders, Fourteenth Amendment and
  A: 112–13, 114

Fenn, Harry
  B: **69–75**, 72 (ill.), 73 (ill.)

Fessenden, William Pitt
  A: 105
  B: 48
  PS: 118

Fields, James T.
  B: 3

Fields, Osgood and Company
  B: 102

Fifteenth Amendment
  A: 23, 52, 144, 160–61
  PS: 54, 94, **165–72**
  Anthony, Susan B., and,
    B: 11–12, 14–15
  celebration over, *PS:* 169, 170 (ill.)
  Civil Rights Act of 1866 and, *PS:* 85
  Douglass, Frederick, and,
    B: 52, 57
  Georgia's readmission to the Union and, *PS:* 130
  Grant, Ulysses S., and, *B:* 81
  Greeley, Horace, and, *B:* 94
  text of, *PS:* 169

Fifth Amendment
  PS: 90

Fifty-fourth Massachusetts regiment
  A: 2, 23, 24, 47
  PS: 55

Fillmore, Millard
  B: 197

Films, African American regiments in
  A: 24
  PS: 55

Financial crises
  Grant, Ulysses S., and, *B:* 82
  Panic of 1837, *B:* 45
  Panic of 1873, *B:* 49 (ill.), 50, 83
  recession, *B:* 50, 83

Financial scandals, Grant, Ulysses S., and
  A: 139

Financing
  American Civil War, *B:* 46–48
  expeditions, *B:* 107
  surveys, *B:* 108

Firelands Historical Society
  B: 45

First Confiscation Act of 1861
  PS: 14

First Reconstruction Act of 1867
  PS: 53, **97–107**

First South Carolina Volunteers
  A: 2, 24, 84 (ill.)

Fish, Hamilton
  B: 82–83, 84–85, 85 (ill.)

Fisk, James
  B: 82
  PS: 174

Fisk University
  A: 197, 202, 204

Florida
  A: 93, 149, 152
  Black Codes in, *PS:* 78
  election of 1876 in, *PS:* 195, 196–97, 201
  election of 2000 in, *PS:* 197
  First Reconstruction Act of 1867 and, *PS:* 102

Florida coast
  B: 72 (ill.)

Flower Fables (Alcott)
  B: 3

Flowers, Andrew
  A: 167, 170

Food Materials and Their Adulterations (Richards)
  B: 165

Ford, Arthur Peronneau
  PS: 3

Ford, Gerald
  B: 36
  PS: 112, 119

Foreign affairs
  B: 82–83, 84–85, 121–22

Foreign-born residents, disenfranchisement of
  PS: 168

Former Confederates. *See also* Confederate leaders
  concerned for future, *PS:* 3
  elected offices and, *PS:* 89, 92–93, 98, 115, 148–49, 155
  pardons, *PS:* 47
  political rights of, *PS:* 89, 148–49, 155
  U.S. Congress and, *PS:* 69, 70

Former slaves. *See also* African Americans; Free African Americans; Slavery; specific former slaves
  behavior of, *A:* 58–59
  bondage after freedom, *PS:* 22
  after Civil War, *PS:* 30–31
  in Civil War, *PS:* 15, 16
  condition of, *PS:* 34, 36
  education and, *A:* 1–2, 3; *PS:* 134
  employment contracts and, *PS:* 58
  freedom's effects on, *A:* 56–65
  interviews with, *A:* 209
  land for, *PS:* 23–25, 31–32, 35–36, 38–39
  as leaders, *A:* 148
  leaving plantations, *PS:* 17–19, 25
  Leigh, Frances Butler, on, *PS:* 62–63
  letters of, *A:* 54–55
  move to Liberia, *PS:* 18
  options for, *PS:* 26

as plantation employees,
  PS: 39, 58, 60, 61,
  62–63, 64
Republican Party and, *PS:*
  134–35
of Sea Islands, *A:* 39–40;
  PS: 24
search for relatives, *PS:*
  25–26, 29–30
white Southerners and,
  PS: 4–5
as workers, *PS:* 64
Forrest, Nathan Bedford
  A: 159, 160 (ill.)
  PS: 160–61, 161 (ill.), 162,
  163, 163 (ill.)
Fort Pillow Massacre
  PS: 160, 163, 163 (ill.)
Fort Sumter
  B: 172
"Forty Acres and a Mule"
  A: 28, 46–47, 52, 68
  PS: 23
Fossils, dinosaur
  B: 105, 107
Foster, Birket
  B: 70
Fourteenth Amendment
  A: 111–15
  B: 140
  PS: 48, 49, 85, **87–96**
African American suffrage
  and, *PS:* 88–89, 166–67
Anthony, Susan B., and,
  B: 11–12
Civil Rights Act of 1866
  and, *PS:* 88
Confederacy members
  and, *B:* 214–15
Douglass, Frederick, and,
  B: 57
Georgia and, *PS:* 74
Greeley, Horace, and, *B:* 94
Plessy v. Ferguson on, *A:* 199
readmission to the Union
  and, *PS:* 53, 93
Reconstruction Acts and,
  A: 126, 131
as "sleeping giant," *PS:* 170
Stephens, Alexander, on
  Georgia and, *PS:* 71–74
Sumner, Charles, and, *B:*
  195

France
  B: 143
*Frank Leslie's Illustrated
  Newspaper*
  B: 70, 171 (ill.)
Franklin Institute
  B: 24
Frazier, Garrison
  PS: 19
Free African Americans. *See
  also* African Americans;
  Former slaves
  A: 35–38
Freedmen's Conventions
  and, *A:* 128–29
in Southern governments,
  A: 171
Free Soil Party
  A: 106
  B: 183, 191
Freed slaves. *See* Former slaves
Freedman's Savings and
  Trust Company
  B: 20, 58
Freedman's Savings Bank
  PS: 44
Freedmen's Aid Societies
  PS: 35–36, 41
Freedmen's Bureau
  A: 45, 45 (ill.), 57, 68–70,
  108–9
  PS: 74
creation of, *PS:* 36–39
education and, *PS:* 41
employment of former
  slaves and, *PS:* 22,
  39–40, 58
Howard, Oliver Otis, and,
  A: 86–87
land distribution and, *A:*
  83–84, 120
Northerners and, *PS:* 42
public school system and,
  PS: 42 (ill.)
U.S. Congress and, *PS:* 17,
  36, 42–43, 49, 84
violence and, *A:* 57 (ill.),
  70; *PS:* 41
work of, *PS:* 39–40
Freedmen's Bureau Act
  PS: **34–45**
conditions leading to
  need for, *PS:* 34–36

Freedmen's Aid Societies
  and, *PS:* 35–36
Johnson, Andrew, and,
  PS: 43, 79, 80 (ill.), 116
text of, *PS:* 37–39
U.S. Congress and, *PS:* 36,
  84
Freedmen's Bureau Bill
  A: 108–9
  B: 186
Freedmen's Conventions
  A: 124, 127–30
Freedom. *See also* Emancipation
  A: 1–26, 19 (ill.), 51–72
  PS: 22, 24, 26–29
abolitionists, *A:* 13–14
African American soldiers
  and, *A:* 20–25
American Civil War be-
  gins, *A:* 16–18
effects of, *A:* 56–65
Emancipation Proclama-
  tion, *A:* 18–20
free African Americans
  and, *A:* 36
Lincoln, Abraham, *A:* 6–7
North vs. South, *A:* 4, 9,
  12, 15–16
obstacles in, *A:* 127
plantation aristocracy, *A:*
  12
Reconstruction era, *A:* 5,
  8–9
rejoicing over, *A:* 52–54,
  189–90
responsibilities of, *A:* 118
slavery conditions before,
  A: 10–11, 13
Freemasons
  B: 182
Frémont, John C.
  B: 92, 197
*From Sunset Ridge: Poems Old
  and New* (Howe)
  B: 131
Fruitlands
  B: 2
Fugitive, Davis, Jefferson, as
  PS: 8
Fugitive Slave Law
  A: 102
  B: 56, 92, 127, 183, 192

Fuller, Margaret
B: 2, 125

G

Gage, Matilda Joslyn
B: 13

Garfield, James A.
A: 183
B: 21, 59–60

Garrison, William Lloyd
A: 14, 14 (ill.), 22
B: 10, 54, 56
PS: 165, 169

Geological Society of Edinburgh
B: 111

Geological Society of London
B: 111

Geological studies
B: 108

Geological Survey of the Territories of the United States
B: 110

Geologische Reichsanstalt of Vienna
B: 111

Geologists
B: 105–12, 111 (ill.)

Geology
B: 106

Georgia
B: 37, 41
African American legislators in, **PS:** 125, 126, 128, 130, 147, 149
African American village in, **A:** 39 (ill.)
African Americans picking cotton in, **A:** 157 (ill.)
black landownership in, **A:** 29, 45–47, 53, 68, 83–85, 120
elections of 1868 and, **A:** 141
First Reconstruction Act of 1867 and, **PS:** 102
Ku Klux Klan in, **PS:** 156

Leigh, Frances Butler, plantation in, **PS:** 58–60, 61–64
letter to Congress from Bullock, Rufus B., and, **PS:** 147–50
"march to the sea" through, **PS:** 3, 5
plantation breakups in, **A:** 158
readmission to the Union, **PS:** 125–26, 128–30
Republican governors in, **PS:** 152
Stephens, Alexander, on Fourteenth Amendment and, **PS:** 71–74
violence against African Americans in, **A:** 177

Gérôme, Jean-Léon
B: 63

Ghettoes
A: 206–7

Gibbs, Jonathan C.
PS: 130

Gibraltar
B: 48

Gideon's Band
A: 28, 29, 40

Glances at Europe (Greeley)
B: 92

Glory
A: 24
PS: 55

"Go west, young man"
B: 95

Gold. *See also* Mining
B: 82, 150
PS: 174

Golden Era
B: 99

Golden Spike ceremony
PS: 176 (ill.)

Goldhurst, Richard
PS: 183

Gone with the Wind (Mitchell)
PS: 151–52

Gordon, John Brown
PS: 1–11, 9 (ill.), 156
on Confederates' despair and hope for future, **PS:** 4–7

on end of the Civil War, **PS:** 1
Ku Klux Klan and, **PS:** 155
as politician, **PS:** 9
wounded in the Civil War, **PS:** 9

Gordon, John Steele
B: 47–48

Gore, Al
PS: 197

Gould, Jay
B: 82
PS: 174

Government bonds
B: 46–48

Governors. *See also* Military governors
African Americans as, **PS:** 132
Bullock, Rufus B., **PS:** 146, 150
of Georgia, **PS:** 146, 152
Hayes, Rutherford B., **B:** 115, 116
Johnson, Andrew, **B:** 136
provisional, **A:** 80
Tilden, Samuel J., **B:** 204
Vance, Zebulon, **B:** 215–16

Goya, Francisco
B: 64

Grand Wizard, of Ku Klux Klan. *See* Forrest, Nathan Bedford

Grant, Ulysses S.
A: 18, 47, 79, 89, 138–39, 139 (ill.)
B: 76 (ill.), **76–88**
PS: 118, 182 (ill.)
Cincinnati Red Stockings and, **B:** 225
Cooke, Jay, and, **B:** 50, 83
corruption and, **A:** 163–64
Douglass, Frederick, and, **B:** 57–58
election of 1868, **A:** 137 (ill.), 137–41; **PS:** 167 (ill.), 167–68, 173
election of 1872, **PS:** 181
end of Reconstruction and, **A:** 179–80
Enforcement Acts and, **A:** 161–62

Fish, Hamilton, and, *B:*
84–85
Greeley, Horace, and, *B:*
95–96, 97
Hayes, Rutherford B., and,
B: 119
Johnson, Andrew, and, *B:*
140, 177
Ku Klux Klan and, *PS:*
156, 163
Lee, Robert E., and, *B:* 80,
174
political cartoons, *A:* 179
(ill.); *B:* 86 (ill.)
Red Cloud, and, *B:* 149,
150, 150 (ill.)
reelection, *A:* 175
salary increase for, *PS:*
183
scandals and, *B:* 204; *PS:*
173–74, 175–77, 181–82
shift in Republican Party
with, *A:* 172
Stanton, Edwin, and, *B:*
80, 173–74, 178
Sumner, Charles, and, *A:*
107; *B:* 197
terms of surrender, *PS:* 1
West Point and, *PS:* 183
Yellowstone National Park
and, *B:* 105, 109
Grant's Tomb
B: 88
Grattan, J. L.
B: 148
Grattan Massacre
B: 148
Great Britain
B: 82–83, 85
Great Depression
A: 205
"The Great Leveler." *See*
Stevens, Thaddeus
Greek War for Independence
B: 126
Greeley, Colorado
B: 96
Greeley, Horace
A: 175, 175 (ill.)
B: 89 (ill.), **89–97**, 93 (ill.),
94 (ill.), 95 (ill.)
Davis, Jefferson, and, *B:*
33, 94

Stephens, Alexander, and,
B: 38
women's suffrage and, *B:* 12
Greeley, Mary
B: 90, 97
Green, John Paterson
PS: **153–64**
"Green Peace"
B: 126
Greenbacks
B: 82
Greeno, C. L.
PS: 8
Grey, William H.
A: 123
Griffith, D. W.
A: 208
Grimes, James W.
PS: 90, 118, 119
Grimké, Angelina
PS: 94
Grimké, Sarah
PS: 94, 95 (ill.)
The Gross Clinic (Eakins)
B: 65 (ill.), 66, 67
Gross, Samuel D.
B: 66
Gump, Forrest
PS: 162

H

Hall, A. Oakey
B: 203
Hall, James
B: 106
Hamer, Thomas L.
B: 77
Hamilton, Alexander
B: 84
Hampton Institute
A: 200, 204
Hampton, Wade
A: 184–85, 185 (ill.)
Hanks, Tom
PS: 162
Hardshells
B: 201
Harnden, Henry
PS: 8
Harney, William S.
B: 148

Harper and Brothers
B: 71
Harper, Ida Husted
B: 15
Harper's Monthly
B: 74
Harper's Weekly
African Americans discuss
politics, *PS:* 53 (ill.)
Civil Right's Bill, *A:* 110
(ill.)
Davis, Jefferson, in, *B:* 156
(ill.)
Freedmen's Bureau, *A:* 57
(ill.)
Johnson, Andrew, im-
peachment of, *PS:* 111
(ill.), 113 (ill.)
Ku Klux Klan, *PS:* 154
(ill.), 159 (ill.)
Memphis riots, *PS:* 99
(ill.)
Panic of 1873, *B:* 49 (ill.)
Revels, Hiram, in, *B:* 156
(ill.); *PS:* 125 (ill.)
Schurz, Carl, as editor of,
A: 91
South Carolina govern-
ment in, *PS:* 136 (ill.)
Harrison, Benjamin
A: 153
B: 17, 21, 60
Harrison, William Henry
B: 92, 182
Harte, Bret
B: 98 (ill.), **98–104**, 103
(ill.)
Harte, Henry
B: 99
Harvard University
A: 202, 204
Hawthorne, Nathaniel
B: 2
Hayden, Ferdinand V.
B: 105 (ill.), **105–12**, 109
(ill.), 111 (ill.)
Hayes, Lucy
A: 182
B: 114, 115, 122
PS: 205–6
Hayes, Rutherford B.
A: 91, 139, 181, 182–83,
183 (ill.), 185–86, 192

B: 113 (ill.), **113–23**
PS: 205 (ill.)
Cardozo, Francis L., and,
  B: 28
Compromise of 1877 and,
  PS: 198, 199, 201
Douglass, Frederick, and,
  B: 59
election of 1876 and, **PS:**
  195–98, 204 (ill.)
Inaugural Address, **PS:**
  195–207, 200 (ill.)
Reconstruction and, **B:**
  41, 118–19
Stephens, Alexander, and,
  B: 39
vs. Tilden, Samuel J., **B:**
  116–18, 117 (ill.), 119,
  199, 204, 206 (ill.),
  206–7
Hendricks, Thomas A.
  B: 204, 205 (ill.)
Herron, Francis J.
  PS: 18–19
Hershaw, Lafayette M.
  A: 204 (ill.)
"High crimes and misde-
  meanors"
  PS: 112
"High-Water Mark" (Harte)
  B: 99
Hinds, James M.
  PS: 156
Hints Toward Reforms (Greeley)
  B: 92
Historians
  on African American
    politicians, **PS:** 122,
    123, 126
  on African American suf-
    frage, **A:** 130
  on carpetbaggers, **PS:** 145
  on corruption in Recon-
    struction era, **A:** 154
  Johnson, Andrew, and, **A:**
    88
  on Ku Klux Klan, **PS:** 155,
    157
  on *The Prostrate State*, **PS:**
    138
  Radical Republicans and,
    A: 108

Reconstruction era and,
  A: 8–9, 147–48
  on Union League, **PS:** 127
*History of the Struggle for
  Slavery Extension or Re-
  striction in the United
  States*
  B: 92–93
History of Woman Suffrage
  (Anthony, et al.)
  B: 15
Holidays, in Southern Unit-
  ed States
  PS: 9–10
Holloway, Houston
  A: 53–54
Home economics
  B: 161, 165, 166, 167
Home Rule
  A: 168
  Greeley, Horace, and, **A:**
    175
  Hayes, Rutherford B., and,
    A: 183, 185–86
  Liberal Republicans and,
    A: 173
Homemaking
  B: 166
Homestead Act of 1862
  A: 78
  B: 135–36
Hood, James
  A: 118
Hoogenboom, Ari
  PS: 195, 196, 197
Hopkins, James, slaves work-
  ing on plantation of
  PS: 23 (ill.)
Horace Greeley Award
  B: 96
Hospital Sketches (Alcott)
  B: 4
Houghton, William Robert
  PS: 135
House Judiciary Committee,
  impeachment process
  and
  PS: 112
Housekeeping
  B: 166
"How I Went Out to Ser-
  vice" (Alcott)
  B: 3

"How Santa Claus Came to
  Simpson's Bar" (Harte)
  B: 102–3
Howard, Oliver Otis
  A: 69, 84, 86–87, 87 (ill.)
  PS: 39, 40 (ill.), 43
Howard University
  A: 87, 197
  PS: 43
Howe, Julia Ward
  B: 124 (ill.), **124–32**
Howe, Samuel Gridley
  B: 125–26, 126 (ill.), 127,
  130
Hughes, Louis
  PS: **22–33**
Human ecology. *See* Home
  economics
Humphreys, Benjamin
  A: 92
Hundred Conventions pro-
  ject
  B: 54
Hunkers
  B: 201
Hurst, Jack
  PS: 161

I

ICY (Institute for Colored
  Youth)
  B: 24, 25
Illiteracy. *See also* Literacy
  and literacy tests
  PS: 106, 123, 142
Illustrators
  B: 69–75
Immigrants
  Chinese, **A:** 163
  disenfranchisement of,
    PS: 168, 169
Immigration, Chinese
  B: 19, 120, 121 (ill.)
Impeachment, of Johnson,
  Andrew. *See also* "Argu-
  ment for the Impeach-
  ment of President John-
  son" (Sumner); Articles
  of Impeachment
  A: 79, 103, 107, 124,
  135–37

B: 140–42, 142 (ill.),
177–78, 187 (ill.),
187–88, 196–97
PS: 84, 111 (ill.), 112–21,
113 (ill.), 118 (ill.)
Inaugural Address (Hayes)
PS: **195–207**, 200 (ill.)
Inauguration
of Hayes, Rutherford B.,
B: 119; *PS:* 200 (ill.)
of Johnson, Andrew, *B:*
137; *PS:* 120
Income taxes
B: 82
Indian Bureau
B: 87, 120–21
Industrial chemistry
B: 165
Insanity, temporary
PS: 206
Institute for Colored Youth
(ICY)
B: 24, 25
Integrated schools
PS: 193
Integration
A: 5, 124, 134, 144, 150
Interracial marriage
B: 60
PS: 55, 81, 82
Intimidation of voters
A: 176–78, 184–85
PS: 88 (ill.), 105–6, 131,
135, 156, 190, 198
Investments
B: 46–51
Ironclad Oath
A: 44
PS: 68
Is Polite Society Polite? (Howe)
B: 131

J

Jack and Jill (Alcott)
B: 6
Jackson, Andrew
A: 78
B: 135, 200
Jackson, Thomas
"Stonewall"
A: 18

Jackson, William A.
PS: 15
Jackson, William Henry
B: 105, 108
James D. Paxton & Company
B: 181
Jay Cooke & Company
B: 46, 47, 48, 49 (ill.), 50,
83
Jefferson, Thomas
B: 137
Jeffersonian
B: 91
Jim Crow laws
A: 183, 186, 190, 195,
198, 201
"John Brown's Body"
B: 127
Johnson, Andrew
A: 35, 78–79, 79 (ill.), 170
B: 133 (ill.), **133–45**, 143
(ill.)
PS: 81 (ill.), 109
African American suffrage
and, *PS:* 46
African Americans and,
PS: 43, 109
during the American Civil
War, *PS:* 108, 113
civil rights and, *A:* 71, 110
**Civil Rights Bill of 1866,
veto of,** *PS:* **77–86**, 116
confiscated Confederate
land and, *PS:* 23,
31–32, 39
Davis, Jefferson, and, *B:*
33; *PS:* 8
disastrous speaking tour,
A: 116–17
Douglass, Frederick, and,
B: 57, 58, 59
elections of 1866 and, *A:*
117
First Reconstruction Act
of 1867 and, *PS:* 104
Fourteenth Amendment
and, *A:* 115
Freedmen's Bureau Bill
and, *PS:* 43, 79, 80 (ill.),
116
Grant, Ulysses S., and, *B:*
80, 177

Greeley, Horace, and, *B:*
95
impeachment of, *A:* 79,
103, 107, 124, 135–37;
B: 140–42, 177–78, 187
(ill.), 187–88, 196–97;
PS: 111 (ill.), 112–21,
113 (ill.), 118 (ill.)
inauguration of, *PS:* 120
Lincoln, Abraham, and,
PS: 108
political cartoons of, *A:*
101 (ill.), 136 (ill.)
Reconstruction and, *A:*
76, 77, 79, 80–82,
85–95, 100, 105, 111,
126; *B:* 137–39, 139
(ill.), 144, 175–76,
184–86, 202–3; *PS:*
46–47, 49, 68–69, 101
Sharkey, William, and, *PS:*
106
speaking tour of, *PS:* 110,
112
Stanton, Edwin, and, *B:*
80, 168, 175–78, 177
(ill.)
Stephens, Alexander, and,
B: 36
Stevens, Thaddeus, and,
B: 180, 184–86, 185
(ill.), 187 (ill.)
Sumner, Charles, and, *B:*
189, 196–97
Surratt, Mary, and, *B:* 174
Tenure of Office Act of
1867 and, *PS:* 111,
116–17
Tilden, Samuel J., and, *B:*
202
U.S. Congress and, *A:* 78,
80, 95, 103, 105, 109,
110, 111, 135–37; *B:* 80,
133, 135, 137–42,
175–78, 184–88; *PS:* 47,
75, 81, 84, 106, 109–13,
120
Vance, Zebulon, and, *B:*
214
Johnson, Lyndon B.
A: 207
Johnston, David Emmons
PS: 144–45

Johnston, Joseph E.
  B: 174
Joint Committee on Recon-
    struction
  A: 108, 110–11
  PS: 47, 70, 71–72, 74,
    100–101
Jones (former slave)
  PS: 156, 157
*Jo's Boys and How They
    Turned Out* (Alcott)
  B: 6, 7
Journal of Home Economics
  B: 167
A Journey in Brazil (Agassiz)
  B: 71
Jubilee of Emancipation
    Proclamation
  A: 204–5
Julian, George W.
  A: 104
Jurors, Civil Rights Bill of
    1875 and
  PS: 186
Justice Department
  PS: 162, 163
Justice system, African
    Americans in
  PS: 43, 78–79, 186

K

Kansas
  B: 148, 193–94
  African American migra-
    tion to, *A:* 197–98; *PS:*
    205
Kansas-Nebraska Act/Bill of
    1854
  A: 6, 106
  B: 192–94
Kansas Freedman's Relief As-
    sociation
  PS: 205
Kearney, Denis
  B: 121 (ill.)
Kellogg, William P.
  A: 181, 184
Kemble, Fanny
  PS: 65–66
Kennedy, John F.
  B: 128

Kennedy, Robert F.
  B: 128
Kentucky
  A: 2, 16, 34
  Emancipation Proclama-
    tion of 1863 and, *PS:* 14
  Fourteenth Amendment
    and, *PS:* 96
  Thirteenth Amendment
    and, *PS:* 17
Keppler, Joseph
  A: 179 (ill.)
Kerner Commission
  A: 207
Key, Barton
  B: 170, 171 (ill.)
Key, Francis Scott
  B: 170, 190
  PS: 206
Key, Philip Barton
  PS: 206
Killing
  by African Americans, *PS:*
    155
  in battle, *PS:* 2, 9
  of carpetbaggers, *PS:* 151
  Forrest, Nathan Bedford,
    and, *PS:* 160, 161, 163
  of Freedmen's Bureau
    agents, *PS:* 41
  by Ku Klux Klan, *PS:* 156,
    160, 161
  Sickles, Daniel E., and, *PS:*
    206
King, Clarence
  B: 108
King, Coretta Scott
  A: 207 (ill.)
King, Edward
  PS: 123
King, Martin Luther, Jr.
  A: 206, 207 (ill.)
Kingdon, Charles
  B: 70
Knickerbocker
  B: 99
Knickerbocker Club
  B: 219, 220
Knights of the Rising Sun
  A: 159
Knights of the White
    Camellia
  A: 159

PS: 156
Koya Oglalas
  B: 147
Kramer, Hilton
  B: 62
Ku Klux Klan
  A: 159–60
  PS: 153, 154 (ill.), 198
  African American officials
    threatened by, *PS:* 130
  African American voters
    and, *A:* 140, 141
  attacking African Ameri-
    cans, *PS:* 135, 153,
    155–56, 159 (ill.)
  beginning of, *PS:* 153–54
  Campbell, John, and, *A:*
    161 (ill.)
  Congress and, *PS:* 160–61
  defenders of, *PS:* 157
  Department of Justice
    and, *PS:* 162
  disbandment of, *PS:*
    160–61, 162
  Flowers, Andrew, and, *A:*
    167
  Forrest, Nathan Bedford,
    and, *PS:* 160–61
  Green, John Paterson, on,
    PS: 156–59
  in late 20th century, *A:*
    207
  political goal of, *PS:* 157
  Union League and, *A:* 132
Ku Klux Klan Act of 1871
  B: 81
  PS: 160–61

L

Labor
  land and, *A:* 67–68, 82–83
  in Reconstruction era
    South, *A:* 38–42, 66–68,
    74–75, 82–83, 156–58
  slave, *A:* 10, 11, 12
Labor contracts
  A: 41, 68, 92, 93
  PS: 39, 58, 78
Labor movement
  A: 164, 205

Labor system, emancipation
and
PS: 3, 4–5
Labor unions
A: 164
Ladd-Franklin, Christine
B: 163
"Lady of the Lake" (Scott)
B: 53
Lakota. *See also* Red Cloud
B: 146, 147, 148, 151
Lamb, A. A., painting by
PS: 13 (ill.)
Land
African American eco-
nomic independence
and, *PS:* 19
claims, *B:* 170
distribution, *PS:* 23–25,
31–32, 35–36
Freedmen's Bureau Act
and, *PS:* 38–39
grants, *B:* 27
labor and, *A:* 67–68,
82–83
leased to African Ameri-
cans, *PS:* 35
redistribution of, *A:* 45–47,
67–68, 83–85, 103,
119–20, 134–35, 150
speculation, *B:* 46
white Southerners and,
PS: 58
Landlord and Tenant Act of
1877
A: 195
Langston, John Mercer
PS: 198 (ill.), 199
Law enforcement
African Americans in, *A:*
152, 196; *PS:* 130
racial riots and, *PS:* 98,
101
white terrorists and, *A:*
160
Lawlessness, in Southern
United States
PS: 4
Lawrence, William B.
B: 84
Laws. *See also* Black Codes;
Legislation

concerning African Amer-
icans, *PS:* 77
of Reconstruction govern-
ments, *A:* 149
segregation, *A:* 150
vagrancy, *A:* 57, 195
Lawyers
Hayes, Rutherford B., *B:*
114–15
Stanton, Edwin, *B:*
169–70, 171 (ill.)
Stevens, Thaddeus, *B:* 181
Tilden, Samuel J., *B:* 201
Le Jeune, Father Paul
B: 147
Lee, Robert E.
A: 18, 47, 139
B: 30 (ill.), 31, **34–36**, 35
(ill.)
PS: 1, 9–10, 59
Grant, Ulysses S., and, *B:*
80, 174
Hayes, Rutherford B., and,
B: 115
"The Legend of Monte del
Diablo" (Harte)
B: 100
Legislation. *See also* Laws;
Southern legislators;
specific legislation
Bland-Allison Act of 1878,
B: 120
Chinese immigration, *B:*
120, 121 (ill.)
Civil Rights Act of 1875,
B: 81
Dawes Act, *B:* 151
Enforcement Act of 1870,
B: 81
Freedmen's Bureau Bill, *B:*
186
homestead, *B:* 135–36
Ku Klux Klan Act of 1871,
B: 81
Reconstruction Act of
1867, *B:* 139
Sherman Silver Purchase
Act, *B:* 50–51
Tenure of Office Act, *B:*
138, 139–42, 176–77,
187–88
Leigh, Frances Butler
PS: 57–66, 65 (ill.)

Lemonade Lucy. *See* Hayes,
Lucy
Lester, John C.
PS: 153–54
***Letter from Rufus B. Bul-
lock, of Georgia, to the
Republican Senators
and Representatives, in
Congress Who Sustain
the Reconstruction
Acts***
PS: **144–52**
Letters
former slave, *A:* 54–55
rejection, Alcott, Louisa
May, and, *B:* 3
Lewinsky, Monica
PS: 112
Liberal Republicans
A: 168, 172–74
B: 96
Liberator
A: 14, 15 (ill.)
B: 54
Liberia
PS: 18
Libraries, public
B: 199, 207
*The Life and Times of Freder-
ick Douglass* (Douglass)
A: 23
B: 60
*The Life and Work of Susan B.
Anthony* (Harper)
B: 15
The Lily
B: 11
Lincoln, Abraham
A: 6–7, 7 (ill.)
PS: 124 (ill.)
African American soldiers
and, *A:* 2, 21
African Americans and, *A:*
48
American Civil War and,
A: 4, 5, 7; *PS:* 13
assassination of, *B:* 33,
174, 175; *PS:* 68
black suffrage and, *A:* 71
Cameron, Simon, and, *B:*
172
Cooke, Jay, and, *B:* 48

Douglass, Frederick, and, *A:* 23; *B:* 56

Emancipation Proclamation of 1863, *A:* 18–19, 31 (ill.); *PS:* 15

Fish, Hamilton, *B:* 84

Freedmen's Aid Societies and, *PS:* 35–36

Grant, Ulysses S., and, *A:* 138; *B:* 78, 79–80

Greeley, Horace, and, *B:* 93–94, 95

homestead legislation and, *B:* 135–36

Johnson, Andrew, and, *A:* 79; *B:* 133, 136, 137; *PS:* 108

political cartoon, *A:* 101 (ill.)

Reconstruction and, *A:* 7, 28, 34, 42–43, 44, 76; *B:* 184; *PS:* 67–68

in Richmond, Virginia, *A:* 47

Schurz, Carl, and, *A:* 90

secession and, *B:* 32, 37

slavery and, *A:* 6–7, 16, 18–19, 20, 30; *PS:* 12, 13, 15, 19–20

Stanton, Edwin, and, *B:* 168, 172–75

Stephens, Alexander, and, *B:* 37

Stevens, Thaddeus, and, *B:* 183–84

Sumner, Charles, and, *B:* 195, 197

Tilden, Samuel J., and, *B:* 201

Toombs, Robert A., and, *B:* 40

Wade-Davis Bill and, *A:* 29, 44

Lincoln High School
B: 25

Liquor, avoidance of
PS: 205–6

Literacy and literacy tests. *See also* Illiteracy
PS: 41, 54, 170, 171

Literary and Theological Review
B: 125

Little Big Horn, Battle of
B: 87, 120, 151

Little Men (Alcott)
B: 6, 7

Little Women (Alcott)
B: 1, 4–8, 5 (ill.)

Little Women or, Meg, Jo, Beth and Amy, Part Second (Alcott)
B: 6

Living conditions, slave
A: 10–11, 11 (ill.), 13

Lobbyists
PS: 182

Log Cabin
B: 91, 92

Logan, John A.
B: 142 (ill.)
PS: 113

Long, Jefferson
A: 151

Long, Thomas
A: 24

Longfellow, Henry Wadsworth
B: 125, 190

Louisa May Alcott: Her Life, Letters, and Journals
B: 2, 7

Louisiana
B: 119, 184
African American suffrage in, *A:* 44
African Americans in law enforcement, *A:* 152
Black Codes in, *A:* 93; *PS:* 77–78
elections of 1868 and, *A:* 141
elections of 1876 in, *A:* 181, 184; *PS:* 195, 196, 201
First Reconstruction Act of 1867 and, *PS:* 102
integrated schools and, *A:* 150
Ku Klux Klan in, *PS:* 156
labor experiments in, *A:* 40–41, 158
Lincoln, Abraham, Reconstruction plan and, *PS:* 68

racial riots in, *A:* 115, 116 (ill.)
Reconstruction of, *A:* 35–38
voter intimidation in, *A:* 162 (ill.)

Louisiana Purchase
A: 15

Loyal Legion of Connecticut
PS: 8

Loyalty oaths
PS: 7, 39, 68

"The Luck of Roaring Camp" (Harte)
B: 100

The Luck of Roaring Camp, and Other Sketches (Harte)
B: 99, 101, 102

Luke, William
A: 160

Lynch, John Roy
A: 151, 152–53, 153 (ill.), 208
B: 156
PS: 131, 187

Lynch law
A: 190, 198

M

Magazines. *See also* specific magazines
Alcott, Louisa May, and, *B:* 3, 4, 7
Grant, Ulysses S., and, *B:* 87
Greeley, Horace, and, *B:* 91, 92
Harte, Bret, and, *B:* 100–102

Mahan, Asa
B: 106

Makhpiya-Luta. *See* Red Cloud

Malcolm X
A: 206

Mammoth Hot Springs
B: 105, 110–11

"The Man of No Account" (Harte)
B: 99

Mansfield Independents
  B: 223
Maps, frontier
  B: 108
"March to the sea"
  PS: 3
Margaret Fuller (Howe)
  B: 130
Marriage
  interracial, *B:* 60; *PS:* 55,
    81, 82
  slavery and, *A:* 11, 59
Marshall, John
  B: 190
Martial law
  A: 65–66
Martin, Edward Winslow
  PS: 173–84
Maryland
  A: 2, 16, 34–35
  Emancipation Proclama-
    tion (1863) and, *PS:* 14
  Fourteenth Amendment
    and, *PS:* 96
  Thirteenth Amendment
    and, *PS:* 17
Masonic Party
  B: 182
Mass media
  B: 91
Massachusetts Anti-Slavery
    Society
  A: 22
  B: 54
Massachusetts Institute of
    Technology (MIT)
  B: 161, 162, 164, 165 (ill.)
Massachusetts regiment,
    Fifty-fourth
  A: 2, 23, 24
  PS: 55
*Max Schmitt in the Single
    Shell* (Eakins)
  B: 64
McCabe, James Dabney. *See*
    Martin, Edward
    Winslow
McClellan, George B.
  A: 18, 20, 79
  B: 48, 172, 173
McCulloch, Hugh
  B: 176

McElrath, Thomas
  B: 91
McGee, Edmund
  PS: 26
McKim, James Miller
  PS: 79
McKinley, William
  A: 153
  B: 17, 21, 138
Media
  B: 91, 92
Meek, Fielding Bradford
  B: 106, 107
Memminger, Christopher
  B: 30 (ill.)
*Memoir of Dr. Samuel Gridley
    Howe … with Other
    Memorial Tributes*
    (Howe)
  B: 125–26, 130
Memphis, Tennessee, racial
    riots in
  A: 115, 159
  PS: 97, 99 (ill.)
Men and Measures (McCul-
    loch)
  B: 176
Merry's Museum
  B: 4, 7
Mexican-American War
  A: 15
  B: 191
  Davis, Jefferson, and, *B:*
    31, 32
  Grant, Ulysses S., and, *B:*
    77–78
  New York Tribune and, *B:* 92
Mexico
  B: 143
  former Confederates in,
    PS: 3, 5
Meyer, Julius
  B: 148 (ill.)
Middle East
  B: 74
Middle Passage
  A: 12
Migration, African American
  to Kansas, *A:* 197 (ill.),
    197–98; *PS:* 205
  to North, *A:* 205
  urban, *A:* 56–57, 82–83,
    205; *PS:* 25, 26

Migration, western
  A: 163
Military arrests
  PS: 103
Military court system
  PS: 79
Military governors
  B: 18, 26–27, 136, 155
Military service
  African Americans and, *B:*
    56–57
  Davis, Jefferson, *B:* 32
  Grant, Ulysses S., *B:*
    77–80
  Hayes, Rutherford B., *B:*
    115
  Lee, Robert E., *B:* 34–36
  Toombs, Robert A., *B:* 40
  Vance, Zebulon, *B:* 212
Militia Act of 1862
  A: 2, 21
Miller, Thomas E.
  A: 164
Mining
  B: 50–51, 100–102, 101
    (ill.)
Ministers, African American
  A: 61, 63
Ministry
  B: 153–55, 159, 160
Minnesota
  B: 148
  African American suffrage
    and, *PS:* 89, 166
Miscegenation
  A: 59, 82
Miss Amelia Van Buren
    (Eakins)
  B: 67
Mississippi
  B: 18–20, 155–56
  African American–run
    community in, *A:* 28,
    41–42
  African Americans in law
    enforcement, *A:* 152
  Black Codes in, *A:* 93; *PS:*
    77
  corruption by govern-
    ment officials, *A:* 156
  education, *A:* 149
  First Reconstruction Act
    of 1867 and, *PS:* 102

Ku Klux Klan in, *PS:* 162
Lynch, John Roy, and, *PS:* 131
Mississippi Plan, *A:* 168, 177–78, 180
pig law in, *A:* 196
political corruption in, *PS:* 124
Second Mississippi Plan, *A:* 191, 199, 202–3
taxes in, *PS:* 145
Thirteenth Amendment and, *PS:* 17
Mississippi Plan
A: 168, 177–78, 180
Mississippi Rifles
B: 32
Mississippi state senate
B: 155–56
Missouri
A: 2, 16, 34
PS: 14, 17
Missouri Compromise of 1820
A: 6, 8 (ill.)
Mistreatment of African Americans
PS: 31, 78
MIT. *See* Massachusetts Institute of Technology (MIT)
Mitchell, Margaret
PS: 151–52
Mitchell, Maria
B: 162, 163
Moderate Republicans
PS: 84, 88–89
Johnson, Andrew, and, *A:* 111
Reconstruction debate and, *A:* 104–5
in Thirty-ninth Congress, *A:* 101
A Modern Mephistopheles (Alcott)
B: 7
Modern Society (Howe)
B: 130
Money, Confederate. *See also* Currency
PS: 9
Monroe, James
PS: 18
Monroe, John T.
B: 187

Montgomery bus boycott (1955)
A: 206
Moods (Alcott)
B: 4
Moore, W. G.
PS: 111 (ill.)
Moorehead, Warren K.
B: 151
Moran, Thomas
B: 105, 109
Morgan, Albert T.
PS: 145
Morgan, Charles
PS: 145
Morgan, J. P.
B: 50
Morton, Oliver P.
A: 117
Moses, Franklin J.
A: 156
Mother's Day
B: 130
Mothers' Peace Day
B: 130
Mott, Lucretia
A: 112
Movies, African American regiments in
A: 24
PS: 55
Mulattoes
A: 36, 124, 128–29
Multiracial democracy
A: 143–44, 147, 150–53, 170–71, 191–92, 193
Multiracial political conventions
A: 133–35
Murder. *See* Killing
Murray, F. H. M.
A: 204 (ill.)
Mutual benefit societies
A: 53, 61, 64
Muybridge, Eadweard
B: 66

N

NAACP (National Association for the Advancement of Colored People)
A: 201, 202

Naduesiu. *See* Lakota
Names, African Americans and
A: 59–60
Narrative of the Life of Frederick Douglass, an American Slave (Douglass)
B: 52, 54–55, 55 (ill.)
PS: 49
Nash, Beverly
PS: 105
Nashville Colored Tennesseean
PS: 25
Nast, Thomas
A: 19 (ill.)
B: 96, 117 (ill.), 156 (ill.), 206 (ill.)
PS: 100 (ill.), 136 (ill.), 178 (ill.)
Nat Batchelor's Pleasure Trip (Alcott)
B: 3
Natchez Board of Aldermen
B: 155
Nation magazine
A: 173–74, 186
National Academy of Design
B: 67, 68
National Academy of Sciences
B: 111
National American Woman Suffrage Association
B: 13, 15, 131
National Association for the Advancement of Colored People (NAACP)
A: 201, 202
National Association of Base Ball Players
B: 220
National Association of Baseball Clubs
B: 218, 223, 224
National bank of United States
B: 200
National Baseball Hall of Fame
B: 218, 220, 221, 223, 224, 224 (ill.)
National Council of Women
B: 60

National League of Professional Baseball Clubs
B: 218, 224
National Negro Business League
A: 201
National parks
B: 105, 109, 110
National Union Party
B: 137. *See also* Republican Party
National Woman Suffrage Association (NWSA)
B: 12, 13, 15, 129
Native Americans. *See also* specific Native Americans
A: 87, 91, 163
Grant, Ulysses S., and, *B:* 87
Harte, Bret, and, *B:* 99–100
Hayden, Ferdinand V., and, *B:* 105, 106
Hayes, Rutherford B., and, *B:* 120–21
leaders, *B:* 148 (ill.)
settlers and, *B:* 147–49
Nebraska
B: 148
"Negro rule"
PS: 131
Nesbitt, George F.
PS: 179, 180
New Departure
A: 168–69, 174
New England Institute for the Blind
B: 125
New England Press Association
B: 96
New England Woman Suffrage Association
B: 129
New Jersey, Fourteenth Amendment and
PS: 93, 96
New National Era
B: 57
New Orleans, Louisiana
A: 35–37
integrated schools and, *A:* 150

racial riots in, *A:* 115, 116 (ill.), 159; *PS:* 97–98
New York Customhouse
B: 119
New York Public Library
B: 199, 207
New York Review
B: 125
New York Stock Exchange
A: 176 (ill.)
B: 50, 83
New York Times
Revels, Hiram, and, *B:* 158
Tilden, Samuel J., and, *B:* 200
Tweed Ring and, *B:* 203
on *Two Men of Sandy Bar: A Drama,* *B:* 103
New York Tribune
A: 54, 175
B: 91–92, 94, 95, 96, 97, 127
New Yorker
B: 90, 91
Newspapers. *See also* specific newspapers
advertisements, *A:* 59
antislavery, *A:* 14, 15 (ill.); *PS:* 49
Fenn, Harry, and, *B:* 70
Greeley, Horace, and, *B:* 89 (ill.), 89–97, 95 (ill.)
Howe, Julia Ward, and, *B:* 126
searching for lost relatives using, *PS:* 25
Nez Perce
B: 87
Niagara Movement
A: 201, 202, 204, 204 (ill.)
Nichols, William R.
B: 164
Niles, Thomas
B: 4, 5
Nineteenth Amendment
A: 113
B: 16
PS: 171
Nixon, Richard
PS: 119
Nkrumah, Kwame
A: 203

North Carolina
A: 93
B: 175–76, 209, 212, 215–16
African American officials in, *PS:* 131
constitution of, *PS:* 151
First Reconstruction Act of 1867 and, *PS:* 102
Ku Klux Klan in, *PS:* 162
North Star
A: 22
B: 52, 55
PS: 49
Northern Californian
B: 99–100
Northern Pacific Railroad
B: 50, 83
Northern Spectator
B: 90
Northern United States
African American migration to, *A:* 205
African American suffrage in, *PS:* 166
African Americans in Union Army, *PS:* 20
Civil War's devastating toll on, *PS:* 2, 3
corruption in, *A:* 154–55
laws concerning African Americans in, *PS:* 85
Reconstruction era developments in, *A:* 162–63
vs. Southern United States, *A:* 4, 9, 12, 15–16
Northerners. *See also* Carpetbaggers
Black Codes and, *PS:* 85
former Confederate congressmen and, *PS:* 70
Freedmen's Bureau and, *PS:* 42
Johnson, Andrew, and, *PS:* 108
on readmission to Union, *PS:* 67
Reconstruction and, *PS:* 98, 102
states' rights and, *PS:* 81
Novels, dime. *See also* specific novels
B: 70–71

Nutrition
B: 166, 167
NWSA. *See* National Woman
Suffrage Association
(NWSA)

O

"O, I'm a Good Old Rebel"
PS: 8–9
Oath of allegiance, by First
South Carolina Volun-
teers
A: 84 (ill.)
Oaths, loyalty
PS: 7, 39, 68
Oberlin College
B: 106
Official holidays, in South-
ern United States
PS: 9–10
Oglalas
B: 147, 148
"Ogontz"
B: 48
Ohio, Fourteenth Amend-
ment and
PS: 93
An Old-Fashioned Girl (Al-
cott)
B: 6
"On Reconstruction"
(Stephens)
PS: 67–76
**"On the Readmission of
Georgia to the Union"**
(Revels)
PS: 122–33
107th Colored Infantry
A: 37 (ill.)
Opium
B: 120
Ordway, John
B: 164
Oregon
B: 148
1876 elections in, *PS:* 195,
196, 201
Oregon Territory
B: 78
Our Young Folks
B: 71

"The Outcasts of Poker Flat"
(Harte)
B: 100–101, 102
Out-of-Doors in the Holy Land
B: 74
*An Overland Journey from
New York to San Francis-
co in the Summer of 1859*
(Greeley)
B: 92
Overland Monthly
B: 98, 100–101
Overseers
A: 10

P

Paine, Lewis
B: 174
Painters
B: 62–64, 66–68
Pale Faces
PS: 156
Paleontology
B: 106
Pan African Congresses
A: 203
Panama Canal
B: 122
Panic of 1837
B: 45
Panic of 1873
A: 169, 175–76, 176 (ill.)
B: 49 (ill.), 50, 83
Paper money, Confederate
PS: 9
Pardons
A: 43, 68, 80, 88
B: 214
PS: 7, 47, 68–69, 75
Paris, Walter
B: 111 (ill.)
Parks, national
B: 105, 109, 110
Parks, Rosa
A: 206
Passion Flowers (Howe)
B: 127
Patrollers
A: 10
"Pattyrollers." *See* Patrollers

Paul Laurence Dunbar High
School
B: 23, 28
Pay
for African American sol-
diers, *PS:* 20
for African American
workers, *PS:* 58, 66
for Grant, Ulysses S., *PS:*
183
for years of slave service,
PS: 32
Peace
Howe, Julia Ward, and, **B:**
130
Native Americans and, **B:**
149
Stephens, Alexander, and,
B: 37–38
Sumner, Charles, on, **B:**
191
Penal code, of Redemption
government
A: 195–96
Pendleton, Leila Amos
PS: 205
Pennsylvania Academy of
the Fine Arts
B: 63, 66, 67
Perdue, Sonny
PS: 152
Periodicals. *See* specific peri-
odicals
Perkinson, Pettus
B: 17–18
*Personal Memoirs of U.S.
Grant* (Grant)
B: 87–88
Philbrick, Edward S.
A: 40
Phillips, Wendell
A: 117
PS: 110
Photography
B: 66
Picturesque America series
B: 69, 71–73, 73 (ill.)
Picturesque Europe
B: 69, 73–74
*Picturesque Palestine, Sinai,
and Egypt*
B: 69, 74

Pierce, Franklin
  B: 31, 32, 197
Pierrepont, Edwards
  A: 178
"Pig law"
  A: 196
Pike, James Shepherd
  PS: 123–24, **134–43**
Pinchback, P. B. S.
  A: 37–38, 38 (ill.)
  PS: 132, 187
Pine Ridge Agency
  B: 151
Pitts, Helen
  PS: 55
"Plain Language from Truthful James" (Harte)
  B: 101
Plantation aristocracy
  A: 12, 85–88
Plantation owners
  PS: 22, 68–69, 109, 113
  Civil War effects on, **A:** 66
  property taxes and, **A:** 150
  in Redemption era South,
    A: 195
  sharecropping and, **A:** 158
  wealth and, **A:** 12
Plantations
  B: 23, 27
  alternatives to African
    American labor for, **PS:**
    65
  breakup of, **A:** 119
  division of, **PS:** 35–36
  former slaves as employees on, **PS:** 39, 58, 60,
    61, 62–63, 64
  former slaves leaving, **PS:**
    17–19, 25, 26
  of Hopkins, James, **PS:** 23
    (ill.)
  house on Southern, **PS:**
    59 (ill.)
  labor experiments on, **A:**
    41–42
  of Leigh, Frances Butler,
    PS: 58–60, 61–64
  post-war, **PS:** 62
  slaves on, **A:** 10, 11, 11
    (ill.)
Planter
  A: 154

Planter aristocracy
  A: 12, 85–88
Plessy, Adolph
  A: 199
Plessy v. Ferguson
  A: 190–91, 198–99
  PS: 54–55, 170, 193
Pocket veto, of Wade-Davis
    Bill
  A: 44
  PS: 68
Poland Committee
  PS: 176, 177–80
Poland, Luke
  PS: 176
Police officers, racial riots
    and
  PS: 98, 101
Political broadside
  PS: 88 (ill.)
Political campaigns
  B: 92
Political cartoons
  African Americans in government in, **PS:** 136
    (ill.)
  anti–African American,
    PS: 191 (ill.)
  Civil Rights Bill in, **A:** 110
    (ill.)
  Crédit Mobilier scandal
    depicted in, **PS:** 178
    (ill.), 181 (ill.)
  Davis, Jefferson, in, **B:** 156
    (ill.)
  election controversy in, **B:**
    117 (ill.), 206 (ill.)
  election of 1868 in, **A:**
    140 (ill.)
  Freedman's Bureau in, **A:**
    45 (ill.)
  Grant, Ulysses S., in, **A:**
    179 (ill.); **B:** 86 (ill.)
  Hayes, Rutherford B., in,
    B: 121 (ill.); **PS:** 204
    (ill.)
  Johnson, Andrew, in, **A:**
    101 (ill.), 136 (ill.); **B:**
    177 (ill.), 185 (ill.); **PS:**
    80 (ill.)
  Lincoln, Abraham, in, **A:**
    101 (ill.)

Stanton, Edwin, in, **B:** 177
    (ill.)
Stevens, Thaddeus, in, **B:**
    185 (ill.)
Thomas, Lorenzo, in, **B:**
    177 (ill.)
Tilden, Samuel J., in, **PS:**
    204 (ill.)
"white man's government" in **PS:** 100 (ill.)
Political conventions, multiracial
  A: 133–35
Political corruption
  Grant, Ulysses S., and, **A:**
    163–64, 179 (ill.)
  in Reconstruction governments, **A:** 153–56, 171,
    192–93
Political organizations
  A: 131, 132
Political parties. *See* specific
    parties
Political rights. *See also* Voting rights
  of former Confederates,
    PS: 89, 148–49, 155
  Fourteenth Amendment
    and, **PS:** 89, 92–93
  Revels, Hiram, on African
    American, **PS:** 126,
    128–30
Politicians. *See* specific
    politicians
Politics
  African Americans and Republican Party, **PS:**
    134–35
  African Americans in, **PS:**
    74, 105–6, 122–24, 125,
    126, 131
  African Americans learn
    about, **PS:** 134
"Politics of livelihood"
  A: 155
Poll tax
  A: 177, 199
  PS: 54, 170, 171
Pope, John
  PS: 117
Population counts
  African Americans and,
    PS: 70, 71, 89

slaves and, *PS:* 12–13, 16, 70

Populism
  A: 202–3

Poverty. *See* Economy

Powell, John Wesley
  B: 108

"The Prayer of Twenty Millions" (Greeley)
  B: 95

Preachers, African American
  A: 61

Preliminary Emancipation Proclamation
  A: 18–19

Presidential election controversy. *See* Election of 1876, controversy

Presidential elections. *See* Elections

Presidential Succession Act of 1792
  PS: 119

Presidential Succession Act of 1947
  PS: 119

Presidents. *See* specific presidents

President's Reconstruction plan
  A: 73–96
  Johnson, Andrew, and, *A:* 76, 77, 79, 80–82, 85–95, 100, 105, 111, 126
  land and labor, *A:* 82–85
  Lincoln, Abraham, and, *A:* 7, 28, 34, 42–43, 76
  opposition to, *A:* 94–95
  Radical Republicans and, *A:* 76–77, 81

Proclamation of Amnesty
  A: 74, 80, 84

Proclamation of Amnesty and Reconstruction
  A: 7, 28, 34, 42–43, 76, 103
  PS: 67–68

Property
  African Americans as, *PS:* 48
  slaves as, *PS:* 14
  voting rights and, *PS:* 151

Property taxes
  A: 150, 194

The Prostrate State (Pike)
  PS: 123–24, **134–43**

Protests, war
  A: 20

Provisional governments
  PS: 104

Public facilities' segregation
  A: 198

Public libraries
  B: 199, 207

Public places, discrimination in
  PS: 185–86, 187–90

Public school systems
  A: 69–70, 149
  B: 182
  Freedmen's Bureau and, *PS:* 41, 42 (ill.)
  Hayes, Rutherford B., on, *PS:* 203
  integration and, *PS:* 193
  in Southern United States, *PS:* 43

Public services, Reconstruction governments and
  A: 148–49

Public transportation, equal access to
  A: 150

Puck magazine
  A: 179 (ill.); *B:* 121 (ill.)

Punch card ballots
  PS: 197

Punishment, of slaves
  A: 10

R

Racial equality. *See* Equal rights

Racial riots
  A: 98, 115, 116 (ill.), 159, 206–7
  PS: 97–98, 99 (ill.)

Racial segregation
  B: 81
  PS: 54–55, 170, 193

Racial tension
  PS: 155

Racial violence. *See* Violence

Racism
  A: 55–56
  PS: 18, 134, 136, 166
  segregation and, *A:* 150
  slaveholders and, *A:* 67
  slavery and, *A:* 4, 13–14
  Union Army and, *A:* 32
  white Southerners and, *A:* 140

Radical Reconstructionists. *See* Radical Republicans

Radical Republicans
  A: 43–44, 71, 170
  B: 137, 175, 180, 189, 195–96, 215
  PS: 84, 88, 109, 168
  Civil Rights Bill and, *A:* 109–10
  elections of 1866 and, *A:* 117
  end of, *A:* 172
  Freedmen's Bureau Bill and, *A:* 108–9
  Johnson, Andrew, and, *A:* 77, 81, 95, 117, 135, 137
  optimism of, *A:* 76–77
  prominent, *A:* 101–4, 106–7
  Reconstruction Acts of 1867 and, *A:* 118–19
  Reconstruction plan of, *A:* 81, 97–121, 123–42, 146
  Southern governments and, *A:* 191
  Union League and, *A:* 132

Railroads
  B: 49–50, 201
  celebrating first transcontinental, *PS:* 176 (ill.)
  corruption and, *PS:* 175–79
  Reconstruction era corruption and, *A:* 156
  segregation of, *A:* 198–99
  U.S. Congress and, *PS:* 174, 177
  western migration and, *A:* 163

Rainey, Joseph
  A: 151

Rainey, Sue
  B: 72

Ransier, Alonzo J.
  A: 209
Rapier, James
  PS: 185–94, 187 (ill.)
Reagan, John
  B: 30 (ill.)
Recollections of the Inhabitants, Localities, Superstitions, and KuKlux Outrages of the Carolinas (Green)
  PS: 153–64
Reconstruction
  African American churches during, *A:* 60–61
  African American politicians during, *PS:* 122–25, 132
  as a bitter period, *PS:* 198
  challenges of, *A:* 5, 8, 98–99
  changing view of, *A:* 8–9
  conflict over, *B:* 137–39, 175–76, 184–86, 202–3
  corruption during, *PS:* 174
  Douglass, Frederick on, *B:* 58–59; *PS:* 49–52
  end of, *A:* 178–80, 183; *B:* 118–19; *PS:* 54
  evaluation of, *A:* 205–9
  failures of, *A:* 190–92
  Grant, Ulysses S., and, *B:* 81–82
  Greeley, Horace, and, *B:* 89, 94–96
  Hayes, Rutherford B., and, *B:* 41, 118–19; *PS:* 198, 199
  Johnson, Andrew, and, *A:* 73–96, 100, 105, 111, 126; *B:* 137–39, 139 (ill.), 144, 175–76, 184–86, 202–3; *PS:* 46–47, 49, 68–69, 101, 106
  Joint Committee on, *PS:* 47, 70, 71–72, 74, 100–101
  key issues in, *B:* 31
  labor and, *A:* 66–68
  legacy of, *A:* 189–210
  Lincoln, Abraham, and, *A:* 7, 28, 34, 42–43, 44, 76; *PS:* 67–68

  overview, *A:* 3–4, 51–52, 143–45
  problems of, *B:* 81–82
  questions concerning, *PS:* 46
  Radical Republicans and, *A:* 81, 97–121, 123–42, 146; *PS:* 109
  readmission of Southern states in, *PS:* 53, 67–68, 98, 101, 102
  rehearsals for, *A:* 33–40
  resentment over taxes during, *PS:* 141
  Stephens, Alexander, on, *PS:* 72–74; *B:* 38
  Stevens, Thaddeus, and, *A:* 102–3; *B:* 175, 184–86
  successes of, *A:* 209
  Sumner, Charles, and, *B:* 175, 189, 195–96
  Tilden, Samuel J., and, *B:* 202–4
  tobacco label depicting, *PS:* 71 (ill.)
  unraveling of, *PS:* 203–5
  U.S. Congress's plan for, *A:* 118; *PS:* 47–48, 53, 68
  Wade-Davis Bill and, *A:* 43–44
"Reconstruction" (Douglass)
  PS: 46–56
Reconstruction Acts of 1867
  A: 118–19, 126, 146
  B: 139
  PS: 74, 84, 147
  First, *PS:* 53, **97–107**, 137, 166
  political activity grows with, *A:* 130–31
  revolutionary effects of, *A:* 120, 143
  state constitutions and, *PS:* 103–4, 105
  Union generals' powers and, *PS:* 105
Reconstruction governments
  achievements and disappointments, *A:* 143–65
  corruption and, *A:* 153–56

  disagreements and tensions in, *A:* 148
  forming of, *A:* 133–35
  multiracial democracy, *A:* 143–44, 147, 150–53, 170–71, 191–92, 193
  Radical Republican's plan for, *A:* 146–47
  Republican goals and achievements in, *A:* 148–49
  white terrorists and, *A:* 159–62
"Reconstruction in South Carolina" (Chamberlain)
  PS: 140
Red Cloud
  B: 146 (ill.), **146–52**, 148 (ill.), 150 (ill.)
Red Cloud Agency
  B: 149
Red Cloud's War
  B: 149–51
Red Shirts
  A: 184, 185
Redemption movement
  A: 167–87, 191, 192–99
  African American disenfranchisement in, *A:* 176–77
  beginnings of, *A:* 171–72
  Compromise of 1877 and, *A:* 183
  elections and, *A:* 176–85
  Hampton, Wade, in, *A:* 184–85
  Hayes, Rutherford B., and, *A:* 185–86
Regiments
  African American, *A:* 2, 23, 24, 36
  Fifty-fourth Massachusetts, *PS:* 55
Regressive tax system
  A: 194
Regulations, labor
  A: 41
Reid, Whitelaw
  PS: 24
  on former slaves and work, *PS:* 64

on Southern states and Constitutional rights, *PS:* 69

on white Southerners, *PS:* 58

Rejection letters, Alcott, Louisa May, and *B:* 3

Relatives, searching for *PS:* 25–26, 29–30

Reminiscences, 1819–1899 (Howe) *B:* 129–30, 131

Reminiscences of the Civil War (Gordon) *PS:* 1–11

Report of the Joint Committee on Reconstruction PS: 100–101

Reports of Cases … in the High Court of Chancery (Sumner) *B:* 191

Republican Party. *See also* Moderate Republicans; Radical Republicans *A:* 15–16, 169

African American voters and, *PS:* 168, 169, 182

convention of 1876, *PS:* 197

debate over Reconstruction in, *A:* 104–5

vs. Democrats, *B:* 116–18, 204, 206–7

election of 1864 and, *B:* 137

in elections of 1866, *A:* 117

in elections of 1867, *A:* 135

in elections of 1868, *A:* 137, 140, 141

in elections of 1874, *A:* 178–80

Fish, Hamilton, and, *B:* 84

former slaves and, *PS:* 134–35

freed African Americans and, *A:* 43–44

Grant, Ulysses S., and, *B:* 80–81, 87

Greeley, Horace, and, *B:* 89, 92, 96

Hayes, Rutherford B., and, *B:* 114–15, 116

impeachment of Johnson, Andrew, and, *PS:* 118–19, 121

Johnson, Andrew, and, *A:* 35, 77, 79

Ku Klux Klan murder, *PS:* 156

Liberal Republicans, *A:* 168, 172–74

Lincoln, Abraham, and, *A:* 6

in Mississippi, *A:* 178

national conventions, *B:* 17, 21, 183

shifting direction of, *A:* 172

slavery and, *B:* 210

in Southern Redemption governments, *A:* 194–95

Stevens, Thaddeus, and, *B:* 183

Sumner, Charles, and, *B:* 192, 197–98

Union League and, *PS:* 127

in U.S. Congress, *A:* 100–101, 104–5, 108

Reunions, family *A:* 59–60 *PS:* 30

Revels, Hiram *A:* 151, 151 (ill.) *B:* 153 (ill.), **153–60**, 156 (ill.), 157 (ill.) *PS:* **122–33**, 125 (ill.)

Revels, Willis *B:* 154

The Reviewers Reviewed (Stephens) *B:* 38

The Revolution B: 13

Revolutionary War *B:* 210

Richards, Ellen H. *B:* 161 (ill.), **161–67**, 165 (ill.)

Richards, Robert Hallowell *B:* 164

Richardson, Albert D. *B:* 71

Richardson, Joe M. *PS:* 130

Richardson, William A. *B:* 83, 86 *PS:* 174

Richmond, Virginia *A:* 47 *PS:* 2 (ill.), 3, 28 (ill.)

Riots. *See also* Racial riots *A:* 20 *B:* 186–87 *PS:* 97–98, 99 (ill.)

Ripley, George *B:* 127

The Rise and Fall of the Confederate Government (Davis) *B:* 34

"The Rival Painters" (Alcott) *B:* 3

The Rival Prima Donnas (Alcott) *B:* 3

Rivers, Prince *A:* 128

Roark, James L. *PS:* 134

Robbers *PS:* 3, 4

Robeson, Eslanda Goode *B:* 24–25

Robeson, Paul *B:* 25

Robson, Stuart *B:* 103

Rogers, Andrew J. *PS:* 90

Roman, Anton *B:* 100, 101

Roosevelt, Theodore *B:* 138

Rose in Bloom (Alcott) *B:* 6

Rosenwald, Julius *A:* 201

Ross, Edmund G. *PS:* 119

Rostenberg, Leona *B:* 4

Runaway slaves. *See also* Fugitive Slave Law *A:* 14, 16–18 *B:* 114, 127

Russia
PS: 120

S

St. George Cricket Club
B: 219
St. Louis, Missouri
A: 197 (ill.)
Salaries. *See* Pay
Santee dialect
B: 147
Santo Domingo
B: 57–58, 83, 84–85, 130
Satirists
B: 98
Saxton, Rufus
A: 83, 84 (ill.), 85, 85 (ill.), 189–90
Scalawags
A: 133, 147, 148, 170–71, 193
historians and, *A:* 8–9
"politics of livelihood" and, *A:* 155
Republican Party and, *A:* 174
Scandals. *See also* Corruption
Crédit Mobilier, *B:* 83
Freedmen's Savings and Trust, *B:* 20
Grant, Ulysses S., and, *A:* 139, 163–64; *B:* 76, 83, 86 (ill.), 86–87; *PS:* 173–74, 175–77, 181–82, 183
in Northern United States, *A:* 154–55
Schools. *See* Education; Public school systems
Schurz, Carl
A: 89–91, 91 (ill.), 108, 172
PS: 48
Scientific American
B: 163
Scientists
Bouchet, Edward, *B:* 24–25
Hayden, Ferdinand V., *B:* 105–12, 111 (ill.)

Mitchell, Maria, *B:* 162, 163
Richards, Ellen H., *B:* 161–62, 163, 164–67, 165 (ill.)
Scott, Robert K.
A: 156
Scott, Sir Walter
B: 53
Scott, Winfield
B: 78
Scribners Monthly, an Illustrated Magazine for the People
B: 110
Sea Islands
A: 29, 38–40, 46
PS: 24
Secession
American Civil War and, *A:* 16
Davis, Jefferson, and, *B:* 32–33
Johnson, Andrew, and, *A:* 77; *B:* 136
Lee, Robert E., and, *B:* 35
map of, *A:* 17 (ill.)
Stephens, Alexander, and, *B:* 37
Sumner, Charles on, *A:* 107
Toombs, Robert A., and, *B:* 40
Vance, Zebulon, and, *B:* 212
Second Confiscation Act of 1862
PS: 14
Second Mississippi Plan
A: 191, 199, 202–3
Second Treaty of Fort Laramie
B: 146
Secretaries of state
B: 27, 28, 84–85
Secretaries of war
Cameron, Simon, *B:* 172
Grant, Ulysses S., *B:* 80, 177
Stanton, Edwin, *B:* 172–78, 177 (ill.)
Segregation. *See also* Plessy v. Ferguson
A: 53, 58–59, 150

B: 81
PS: 54–55, 170, 193
accommodation to, *A:* 200–201
Jim Crow laws, *A:* 195, 198
in schools, *A:* 134
Selling, of slaves
A: 10–11
Selma to Montgomery, Alabama, march
A: 207 (ill.)
Senators. *See also* specific senators
Alcorn, James Lusk, *B:* 19
Blanche, Bruce K., *B:* 17–22
Conkling, Roscoe, *B:* 19
Johnson, Andrew, *B:* 144
Revels, Hiram, *B:* 156 (ill.), 156–59, 157 (ill.)
Sumner, Charles, *B:* 192–97
Vance, Zebulon, *B:* 209, 214, 216
Seneca Falls Convention of 1848
PS: 55, 95
"Separate but equal"
A: 206
PS: 170, 193
The Sermon on the Mount
B: 74
Settle, Thomas
A: 133
B: 215
Settlers, Native Americans and
B: 147–49
Seward, William H.
B: 91, 143
PS: 80, 93
Sexual violence
A: 59
Seymour, Horatio
A: 137, 137 (ill.), 140 (ill.), 141
B: 81
PS: 167 (ill.), 168
Sharecropping
A: 132, 145, 157–58, 194, 195
PS: 22, 26
Sharkey, William
PS: 106

Shaw, Robert Gould
  A: 24
Sheridan, Philip
  A: 115, 135
  PS: 98, 117
Sheriffs, African Americans as
  PS: 130
Sherman, John
  A: 105
"Sherman land"
  A: 46, 53, 68
Sherman Silver Purchase Act
  B: 50–51
Sherman, William T.
  A: 30, 41–42
  B: 174
  on Freedmen's Bureau, A:
    69
  Howard, Oliver Otis, and,
    A: 86; PS: 39
  land distribution and, PS:
    23, 31–32
  "march to the sea" by, PS:
    3
  Special Field Order #15
    and, A: 29, 45–47, 53,
    68, 83, 120
Sickles, Daniel E.
  B: 170, 171 (ill.)
  PS: 117, 195, 206
Silver
  B: 50–51
Sioux. See Lakota
Sitting Bull
  B: 148 (ill.)
Sixteenth Amendment
  B: 129
Slaughterhouse Cases
  A: 169, 180
Slaveholders
  A: 36, 54–56, 67
Slavery. See also Abolition-
    ists; Emancipation; For-
    mer slaves
  A: 170
  Africa and, PS: 20
  Alcott, Louisa May, and,
    B: 3
  American Civil War and,
    A: 4–5, 17, 18–20, 30,
    51; PS: 3, 13
  Anthony, Susan B., and,
    B: 9

Avery, Charles, and, B: 26
Blanche, Bruce K., and, B:
  17–18
bondage after freedom,
  PS: 26, 27–29
Cardozo, Francis L., and,
  B: 27
conditions under, A: 13
Davis, Jefferson, and, B:
  32
Democrats and, B: 201
division over, A: 4–5,
  15–16
Douglass, Frederick, and,
  B: 52–57
economy based on, A:
  12–13
education of slaves, A: 64
end of, A: 30–31, 44,
  51–72, 97; PS: 3, 12, 14
  (ill.), 14–17, 19–20, 165
escape to the North, PS:
  14–15, 16
expansion of, A: 6, 8 (ill.),
  15
Greeley, Horace, and, B:
  92, 93–94
hardships after, PS: 34
homestead legislation
  and, B: 135–36
Howe, Julia Ward, and, B:
  126–27
Johnson, Andrew, and, A:
  35, 78, 81–82
legal in U.S. Constitution,
  PS: 12–13, 16
Leigh, Frances Butler, and,
  PS: 59
in Liberia, PS: 18
Lincoln, Abraham, and,
  A: 6–7, 16, 18–19, 20,
  30; PS: 12, 13, 19–20
living conditions of
  slaves, A: 10–11, 11
  (ill.), 13
Louisiana and, A: 36–37
marriage and, A: 11, 59
Maryland and, A: 34
picking cotton, PS: 60
  (ill.)
on plantation, PS: 23 (ill.)
racism and, A: 4, 13–14

runaway slaves, A: 14,
  16–18; B: 114, 127
slaves as property, PS: 14
slaves in Confederate
  army, PS: 20
slaves in Union Army, A:
  17–18, 28, 32, 82–83
Stevens, Thaddeus, and,
  A: 102; B: 180, 182, 183
Sumner, Charles, and, A:
  106–7; B: 189, 192–94,
  195; PS: 114
taxes and, PS: 142
"three-fifths compromise"
  and, PS: 12
Toombs, Robert A., and,
  B: 39–40
Slippery Dick. See Connolly,
  Richard B.
Smalls, Robert
  A: 128, 151, 154–55, 155
  (ill.), 189, 209
Smith, James M.
  A: 177
Social equality
  PS: 187
Social services
  of African American
    churches, A: 63
  Freedmen's Bureau and,
    A: 87
  in multiracial democratic
    South, A: 171
  Reconstruction govern-
    ments and, A: 134
Société Impériale of Moscow
  B: 111
Society of Illustrators
  B: 75
Soft money
  B: 120
Softshells
  B: 201
Soldiers
  PS: 15, 20, 124 (ill.)
  African American, A: 2,
    20–25, 36, 37 (ill.)
Song lyrics, for "O, I'm a
  Good Old Rebel"
  PS: 8–9
The Song of the Sower
  (Bryant)
  B: 74

Sons of Temperance
  B: 11
Soule, John
  B: 95
The Souls of Black Folk
  (Du Bois)
  A: 202
South America, former Con-
  federates in
  PS: 3, 5
South Carolina
  A: 47
  B: 27, 119, 212
  African American
    landownership in, *A:*
    29, 46–47, 53, 68,
    83–85, 120, 150
  African Americans in poli-
    tics, *A:* 152–53
  Black Codes in, *A:* 93; *PS:*
    47, 78
  constitution of, *PS:* 151
  Constitutional Conven-
    tion, *B:* 27
  education in, *A:* 149
  elections of 1876 in, *A:*
    184–85; *PS:* 195, 196,
    201
  elections of 1878 in, *PS:*
    206
  First Reconstruction Act
    of 1867 and, *PS:* 101–4
  freed slaves on Sea Islands
    of, *PS:* 24
  Ku Klux Klan in, *PS:* 156,
    161–62
  plantation breakups, *A:*
    158
  prewar conditions, *A:* 149
  Reconstruction govern-
    ment's budget, *A:* 150
  state constitution of, *PS:*
    141
South Carolina legislature
  African Americans in, *PS:*
    131, 135–36, 141
  after the Civil War, *PS:*
    137 (ill.), 138–40
  Pike, James Shepherd, on,
    PS: 136–40
  political cartoon of, *PS:*
    136 (ill.)

South Carolina Volunteers,
  First
  A: 2, 24, 84 (ill.)
Southern Democrats. *See*
  also Democratic Party
  A: 193–95
  corruption by, *A:* 156
  economy and, *A:* 171, 176
  in elections of 1872, *A:* 174
  vs. Radical Republicans,
    A: 146
Southern legislators
  federal government par-
    ticipation by, *A:* 111
  Thirty-ninth Congress
    and, *A:* 105
Southern soldiers. *See* Confederate troops
Southern United States. *See*
  also Confederacy; Re-
  construction; Redemp-
  tion movement
  African American
    landownership in, *A:*
    45–47, 67–68, 83–85,
    103, 119–20, 134–35,
    150
  African American rights
    and, *PS:* 54–55, 71, 72
  African Americans in poli-
    tics and government, *A:*
    61, 63, 150–53, 155
  Black Codes in, *A:* 91–94;
    PS: 19, 47, 49, 69–70,
    77–78, 80–81, 85
  carpetbaggers, *PS:* 144–46,
    147
  as a changed society, *A:*
    73–76
  after the Civil War, *PS:*
    2–3, 5, 9, 57–58, 60, 61,
    63–64
  debt in, *PS:* 89, 93,
    140–41, 151
  desolation in, *A:* 66,
    73–74
  economy of, *A:* 4, 13,
    66–67, 104, 156, 171,
    174, 176, 196
  elections in, *A:* 88, 135,
    140–41, 174, 176–85;
    PS: 105, 135, 195–98

federal government par-
    ticipation and, *A:* 111
  federal troops in, *PS:* 74,
    198, 201, 203
  Fourteenth Amendment
    and, *A:* 112–13, 115
  Freedmen's Conventions
    in, *A:* 127–30
  Hayes, Rutherford B., *In-*
    augural Address and, *PS:*
    199, 201–3
  honoring war heroes, *PS:*
    9–10
  Johnson, Andrew, and, *PS:*
    46–47, 49, 68–69, 101
  labor and, *A:* 4, 38–42,
    66–68, 74–75, 156–58
  lawlessness after the Civil
    War, *PS:* 4
  Lincoln, Abraham, and,
    A: 6–7; *PS:* 67–68
  mistreatment of African
    Americans in, *A:* 129,
    140
  multiracial democracy in,
    A: 170–71, 191–92, 193
  new social order, *PS:* 3,
    4–5
  vs. Northern United
    States, *A:* 4, 9, 12,
    15–16
  options for freed slaves,
    PS: 26
  political rights of former
    Confederates, *PS:* 89
  provisional governments,
    PS: 104
  public school system in,
    A: 69–70; *PS:* 43
  readmission to Union, *PS:*
    53, 67–68, 93, 98, 101,
    102, 103, 148
  Reconstruction as bitter
    period, *PS:* 198
  Reconstruction challenges
    in, *A:* 5
  Reconstruction expendi-
    tures, *PS:* 140–41
  Reconstruction govern-
    ments in, *A:* 133–35,
    141, 143–65
  reports on conditions in,
    A: 89–92, 108, 110–11

Republican Reconstruction plan for, *A:* 118–19, 126

slaves in, *A:* 10–11, 12, 13; *PS:* 20

taxes in, *PS:* 7, 141, 142, 151

Thirteenth Amendment and, *PS:* 17

Union League and, *A:* 132

Union's African American soldiers and, *A:* 25

U.S. Congress's Reconstruction plan for, *PS:* 47–48, 49, 53

violence against African Americans in, *A:* 58, 70, 89, 129, 140, 159, 160, 171, 181 (ill.)

wealth in, *A:* 12

white terrorists in, *A:* 158–60

Spain
B: 85

Spanish painters
B: 64

Sparks, Eliza
A: 27

Special Field Order #15
A: 29, 45–47, 53, 68, 83, 120

Speight, Jesse
B: 32

Spittoons
PS: 141

Sports champions
B: 225

Spotted Tail
B: 148, 148 (ill.)

Springfield Republican
B: 100

Spy Vanity Fair
B: 103 (ill.)

Stalwarts
A: 172–73

Stanbery, Henry
PS: 105

Stanton, Edwin
A: 46, 119, 135, 172
B: 80, 139–42, 168 (ill.), **168–79**, 177 (ill.)
PS: 19, 110–11, 117, 118

Stanton, Elizabeth Cady
A: 111 (ill.), 112, 113, 114
B: 11, 12–13, 13 (ill.), 14 (ill.), 129, 131
PS: 95

Stanton, Henry
B: 12

"Star-Spangled Banner" (Key)
B: 170, 190

State constitutions
carpetbaggers and, *PS:* 151
Reconstruction Acts of 1867 and, *PS:* 103–4, 105
Reconstruction era South and, *A:* 119, 126, 146; *PS:* 53
South Carolina, *PS:* 141
Thirteenth Amendment and, *PS:* 17

State of Pennsylvania vs. Wheeling and Belmont Bridge Company
B: 169

States' rights
PS: 50–51, 81

Stearns, Marcellus Lovejoy
PS: 196

Stephens, Alexander
A: 88
B: 30 (ill.), 30–31, **36–39**, 37 (ill.)
PS: **67–76**, 70 (ill.)

Stereotypes, of African American politicians
PS: 123–24, 126

Stevens & Paxton
B: 181

Stevens, Thaddeus
A: 76, 102–3, 103 (ill.), 104, 172
B: 137, 142 (ill.), 175, 180 (ill.), **180–88**, 185 (ill.), 187 (ill.), 195
PS: 19, 87, 91, 110, 112, 113 (ill.)
Johnson, Andrew, and, *A:* 103, 117
Southern land redistribution and, *A:* 120

Stock market
B: 50, 82, 83

Stock market panic (1869)
PS: 174

Stocks, Crédit Mobilier scandal and
PS: 175, 177–80

Stockton, John Potter
B: 158

Stone, John M.
B: 160

Stone, Kate
PS: 58

Stone, Lucy
B: 129

Store owners, cheating African Americans
PS: 65

Story, Joseph
B: 190

The Story of the Fountain (Bryant)
B: 74

Strikes
B: 120

Studies at Home
B: 166

Suffrage. *See* African American suffrage

Sumner, Charles
A: 76, 104, 106–7, 107 (ill.), 172, 180
B: 189 (ill.), **189–98**
PS: 110 (ill.), 124 (ill.)
as abolitionist, *PS:* 114
argument for impeachment of Johnson, Andrew, *PS:* 108–21
Brooks, Preston S., assaults, *B:* 193 (ill.), 194; *PS:* 120
Howe, Julia Ward, and, *B:* 125
Johnson, Andrew, and, *PS:* 110
racial equality and, *PS:* 185–87
Reconstruction and, *B:* 137, 175, 189, 195–96
Revels, Hiram, and, *B:* 158
Stanton, Edwin, and, *B:* 178
Thirteenth Amendment and, *B:* 11

Sumner, Charles Pinckney
B: 190
Sun Pictures of Rocky Mountain Scenery
B: 107
Sun spots
B: 163
"Sunlight" (Alcott)
B: 3
Suppression clauses, of Second Mississippi Plan
A: 199
Supreme Court. *See* U.S. Supreme Court
Surratt, John, Jr.
B: 174
Surratt, Mary
B: 174
Surveys
B: 106–10
Sweeny, Peter Barr
B: 203
Swift Bear
B: 148 (ill.)
"Swing around the circle"
A: 116
PS: 110, 112
Sylvester's Bank Note and Exchange Manual
B: 90

T

Tappan, Benjamin
B: 169
Taxes
B: 82, 86–87
African Americans and, **PS:** 78
to fund Freedmen's Bureau, **PS:** 42
in Mississippi, **PS:** 145
poll, **A:** 177, 199; **PS:** 54, 170, 171
in Reconstruction, **A:** 150, 194
in Reconstruction era South, **PS:** 7, 141, 142, 151
for social services, **A:** 171
Taylor, Zachary
B: 32, 78, 191

Teachers. *See also* Education
B: 10, 25–26
Temperance
B: 9, 11, 122
PS: 205–6
Temporary insanity
B: 170
PS: 206
Ten Per Cent Plan. *See also* Proclamation of Amnesty and Reconstruction
B: 184
Ten Years on a Georgia Plantation Since the War (Leigh)
PS: 57–66
Tennessee
A: 35
B: 136
PS: 68, 69–70, 93
Confederacy and, **A:** 78–79
Fourteenth Amendment and, **A:** 115
racial riots, **A:** 115
white terrorists, **A:** 159, 160
Tennessee House of Representatives, Johnson, Andrew in
B: 135
Tennyson, Alfred, Lord
B: 74
Tenure of Office Act (1867)
A: 135, 136
B: 138, 139–42, 176–77, 187–88
PS: 111, 116–17, 121
Terrorism
PS: 78, 98, 153, 156–57, 162
Teton dialect
B: 147
Teton Sioux
B: 150
Texas
A: 93, 149, 159, 160
First Reconstruction Act of 1867 and, **PS:** 102
Thieves
PS: 3, 4

Thirteenth Amendment
A: 7, 44, 75, 109
B: 11, 57, 138
PS: 12–21
Thirty Years a Slave: From Bondage to Freedom (Hughes)
PS: 22–33
Thirty-ninth Congress
A: 95, 100–101, 104–6, 117–18
Thomas, Lorenzo
B: 177 (ill.), 178
PS: 111, 117
Thompson, Julius E.
B: 159
Thoreau, Henry David
B: 2
"Three-fifths compromise"
PS: 12–13, 16
Through Five Administrations: Reminiscences of Colonel William H. Crook (Crook)
B: 173
Ticknor and Fields
B: 71
Ticknor, Anna
B: 166
Tilden, Elam
B: 199–200
Tilden, Samuel J.
A: 180 (ill.), 181, 183
B: 199 (ill.), **199–208**
PS: 195, 201, 204 (ill.)
on election of 1876, **B:** 39
vs. Hayes, Rutherford B., **B:** 116–18, 117 (ill.), 119, 204, 206 (ill.), 206–7
Hendricks, Thomas A., and, **B:** 204, 205 (ill.)
Tillman, Benjamin R.
A: 185, 203
Tilton, Theodore
PS: 69, 93
"To Thine Own Self Be True"
A: 110 (ill.)
Tobacco label, depicting Reconstruction
PS: 71 (ill.)

Toombs, Robert A.
  B: 30 (ill.), 31, 37, **39–41,**
    40 (ill.)
Tourgée, Albion W.
  PS: 145–46
The Tragic Era (Bowers)
  B: 208
Training facilities, teacher
  B: 25–26
*Transactions of the Kansas
    State Historical Society*
  B: 151–52
Transcontinental railroad
  PS: 175–80, 176 (ill.)
Treason, Stephens, Alexan-
    der, and
  PS: 75
Treasury Department
  B: 21, 48
Treaties
  annexation, *B:* 83, 84
  with China, *B:* 120
  with Great Britain, *B:*
    82–83, 85
  Native Americans and, *B:*
    146, 148, 149
Treaty of Washington
  B: 82–83, 85
Trelease, Allen W.
  PS: 127
"A Trip to Cuba" (Howe)
  B: 127
Trotter, William Monroe
  A: 204 (ill.)
Trowbridge, John Townsend
  PS: 23–24, 58 (ill.)
  on corruption in Freed-
    men's Bureau, *PS:* 40
  on destruction in South,
    PS: 57–58
  on schools for African
    Americans, *PS:* 41
Trumbull, Lyman
  A: 105, 108
  PS: 43, 79
Turner, Henry McNeal
  PS: 125, 192–93
Tuskegee Institute
  A: 200, 201, 204
Twain, Mark
  B: 87, 103, 104 (ill.)
Tweed Ring
  B: 202–4

Tweed, William Marcy
    "Boss"
  B: 202, 203, 203 (ill.)
  PS: 174
Twenty-fifth Amendment
  PS: 119
Twenty-first Amendment
  PS: 206
Twenty-fourth Amendment
  PS: 171
*Two Men of Sandy Bar: A
    Drama* (Harte)
  B: 103
Tyler, John
  B: 144

U

Uncle Horace. *See* Greeley,
    Horace
Uncle Sam
  B: 117 (ill.)
Under the Lilacs (Alcott)
  B: 6
Underground Railroad
  A: 14
  B: 26, 54, 55–56
Understanding clauses
  A: 199
Union army. *See also* Ameri-
    can Civil War; specific
    regiments
  B: 78, 79, 80, 107, 155
  African Americans in, *A:*
    2, 20–25
  slaves and, *A:* 17–18, 28,
    32, 82–83
  Smalls, Robert, and, *A:*
    154
Union League
  A: 125, 131, 132
  PS: 127
Union Pacific railroad com-
    pany
  PS: 175, 177
Union, readmission to
  B: 27, 137–38, 140
  PS: 148
  Congress's plan for, *PS:*
    68, 101
  debate over, *PS:* 67, 98,
    102

First Reconstruction Act
    of 1867 and, *PS:* 53,
    101, 103
  Fourteenth Amendment
    and, *PS:* 93
  Georgia and, *PS:* 125–26,
    128–30
  Johnson, Andrew, plan
    for, *PS:* 68
  Lincoln, Abraham, plan
    for, *PS:* 67–68
  Stephens, Alexander, on
    Georgia's, *PS:* 71–74
Union troops
  African Americans as, *PS:*
    15
  providing for Southern
    African Americans, *PS:*
    34–35, 36
  slaves and, *PS:* 14, 29
  violence against, *PS:* 69
Unionists
  A: 193–94
  Johnson, Andrew as, *A:*
    81–82
  in Louisiana, *A:* 36–37
  in Maryland, *A:* 34
Unions, labor
  A: 164
Unitarians
  B: 128 29
United States. *See also*
    Southern United States;
    U.S. Congress; U.S.
    Supreme Court; specific
    departments and events
  border states, *A:* 2
  vs. Great Britain, *B:*
    82–83, 85
  secession from, *A:* 17 (ill.)
  vs. Spain, *B:* 85
United States v. Cruikshank
  A: 180
Universities. *See* Colleges
    and universities
University of California
  B: 101
Up from Slavery (Washing-
    ton)
  A: 201
Urban migration
  A: 56–57, 82–83, 205
  PS: 25, 26

A = Reconstruction Era: Almanac   B = Reconstruction Era: Biographies

U.S. Bureau of Indian Affairs
B: 87, 120–21

U.S. Congress
African Americans and, *A:*
71; *PS:* 47
Black Codes and, *PS:* 48,
49, 87, 91
Bullock, Rufus B., letter
to, *PS:* 146, 147–50
corruption and, *PS:* 174
debates readmission of
Southern states, *PS:* 98
end of slavery and, *PS:* 15,
16 (ill.), 17
First Reconstruction Act of
1867 and, *PS:* 101, 104
former Confederates in,
PS: 69, 70
Fourteenth Amendment
and, *PS:* 88–91
Freedmen's Bureau and,
PS: 36, 42–43, 84
Freedmen's Conventions
and, *A:* 130
Georgia's readmission to
the Union and, *PS:*
125–26, 130
Hayden, Ferdinand V.,
and, *B:* 109, 110
Hayes, Rutherford B., in,
B: 115; *PS:* 197
Johnson, Andrew, and, *A:*
78, 80, 95, 103, 105,
109, 110, 111, 135–37;
B: 80, 133, 135, 137–42,
175–78, 184–88; *PS:* 47,
75, 81, 84, 106, 109–13,
120
presidential succession
policy and, *PS:* 119
railroads and, *PS:* 174, 177
Reconstruction plan of,
PS: 47–48, 49, 68
Republican majority in, *A:*
100–101, 104–5, 108;
PS: 84
response to *Report of the
Joint Committee on Re-
construction, PS:* 74
Revels, Hiram, first speech
to, *PS:* 126, 128–30
runaway slaves and, *A:* 18
slaves and, *PS:* 14

Stephens, Alexander, in,
B: 38–39
Stevens, Thaddeus, in, *A:*
102–3; *B:* 183–88
struggle with Reconstruc-
tion plan, *A:* 118
testimony about Ku Klux
Klan to, *PS:* 155
Toombs, Robert A., in, *B:*
39–40
Vance, Zebulon, and, *B:*
211–12, 214–15

U.S. Constitution. *See also*
specific amendments
amending process, *PS:* 15
impeachment process
and, *PS:* 112
slavery in, *PS:* 12–13, 16

U.S. currency. *See* Currency

U.S. Department of Agriculture
B: 167

U.S. Department of Defense
B: 172
Freedmen's Bureau Act
and, *PS:* 36, 37

U.S. Department of Justice
PS: 162, 163

U.S. Department of the Interior
B: 108

U.S. Department of the Treasury
B: 21, 48

U.S. Geological Survey for
the Territories
B: 108

U.S. House of Representa-
tives. *See also* U.S. Congress
Civil Rights Bill of 1875
and, *PS:* 187–90
Elliott, Robert Brown, in,
PS: 122–23, 124 (ill.)
Fourteenth Amendment
and, *PS:* 91
impeachment process
and, *PS:* 112
Thirteenth Amendment
and, *PS:* 12, 15, 16 (ill.)

U.S. Military Academy at
West Point
PS: 183

U.S. Sanitary Commission
B: 127

U.S. Senate. *See also* U.S.
Congress
Civil Rights Bill of 1875
and, *PS:* 187
Fourteenth Amendment
and, *PS:* 91
impeachment of Johnson,
Andrew, *PS:* 113, 113
(ill.), 117–18
impeachment process
and, *PS:* 112
Johnson, Andrew, in, *PS:*
120
Thirteenth Amendment
and, *PS:* 12, 15

U.S. Supreme Court
*Brown v. Board of Educa-
tion, A:* 199, 206; *PS:*
193
Civil Rights Act of 1875
and, *PS:* 85, 191–93,
205
Dred Scott decision, *PS:* 79
election of 2000 and, *PS:*
197
Plessy v. Ferguson, A:
190–91, 198–99; *PS:*
54–55, 170, 193
Slaughterhouse Cases, *A:*
169, 180
Tenure of Office Act
(1867) and, *PS:* 121

V

Vagrancy
A: 53, 57, 93, 195
Van Buren, Martin
B: 92, 200
Vance, Robert Brank
B: 210
Vance, Zebulon
B: 209 (ill.), **209–17**
Vandals
PS: 4
Vassar College
B: 162, 163
Vassar, Matthew
B: 163

Velázquez, Diego
  B: 64
Veto
  of Civil Rights Bill (1866),
    A: 110; **PS:** 77, 79,
    80–84, 109
  of First Reconstruction
    Act (1867), **PS:** 104, 109
  of Freedmen's Bureau Bill,
    A: 109; **PS:** 43, 79, 80
    (ill.), 109
  of Tenure of Office Act
    (1867), **PS:** 111
  of Wade-Davis Bill (1864),
    PS: 68
Vickers, George
  B: 158
Vicksburg, surrender of
  B: 79, 79 (ill.)
Violence. *See also* Killing
  against African Ameri-
    cans, **PS:** 69, 78, 97–98,
    99 (ill.), 101, 105–6,
    130, 155–56, 159 (ill.)
  by African Americans, **PS:**
    155
  against carpetbaggers, **PS:**
    151
  in elections, **A:** 176–78
  Freedmen's Bureau and,
    A: 57 (ill.), 70
  against Freedmen's Bureau
    agents, **PS:** 41
  intimidation in elections
    and, **PS:** 105–6, 156,
    190
  in late twentieth century,
    A: 207
  sexual, **A:** 59
  against Southern African
    Americans, **A:** 58, 70,
    89, 129, 140, 159, 160,
    171, 181 (ill.)
  Union League and, **PS:**
    127
  against Union soldiers,
    PS: 69
  by white terrorists, **A:**
    159–60
Virginia
  PS: 68, 102, 151
  Lee, Robert E., and, **B:**
    35–36

Virginius
  B: 85
Vocational education
  A: 200–201, 204
Voting rights. *See also*
    African American suf-
    frage; Women's suffrage
  A: 5, 23, 194–95
  B: 15, 16, 57
  African Americans and,
    PS: 46, 52, 53–54, 88
    (ill.), 100 (ill.), 106,
    156, 166, 170, 190, 192
    (ill.), 203–5
  in District of Columbia,
    A: 117
  in elections of 1872, **A:**
    175
  in elections of 1874, **A:**
    177–78
  Enforcement Acts and, **A:**
    160–62
  of European immigrants,
    PS: 168
  of former Confederates,
    A: 134, 146; **PS:** 89, 155
  Fourteenth Amendment
    and, **PS:** 89, 91, 92,
    166–67
  fraud and, **PS:** 196, 206
  Grant, Ulysses S., and, **A:**
    139
  literacy tests and, **PS:** 170,
    171
  property and, **PS:** 151
  Reconstruction Act of
    1867 and, **PS:** 53, 101,
    104, 166
  in Redemption era South,
    A: 176–77
  Second Mississippi Plan
    and, **A:** 199
Voting Rights Act
  A: 206

W

Wade, Benjamin F.
  A: 44, 104
  PS: 118–19, 121
Wade-Davis Bill
  A: 29, 43–44

PS: 68
Waite, Morrison R.
  B: 119
  PS: 200 (ill.)
Wallace, John
  PS: 196–97
Wallowa Valley
  B: 87
War bonds
  B: 46–48
War Department
  B: 172
  Freedmen's Bureau Act
    and, **PS:** 36, 37
War heroes
  PS: 9–10
Ward, Samuel, Jr.
  B: 125
Warmoth, Henry Clay
  PS: 132
Warren, Gouverneur K.
  B: 107
Washington, Booker T.
  A: 200–201, 201 (ill.), 202,
    203–4
Washington, Denzel
  PS: 55
Washington, George
  A: 139
  B: 80, 210
Washington, Martha
  B: 34
Watergate scandal
  PS: 119
Watts riots
  A: 207
Wayne, Anthony
  PS: 182
Webb, Lucy. *See* Hayes, Lucy
Webster, Alexander Hamilton
  B: 36
Webster, Daniel
  B: 190
Weed, Thurlow
  B: 91
Weekly Tribune
  B: 92
West
  black suffrage in, **A:** 118
  migration to, **A:** 163
  Reconstruction era devel-
    opments in, **A:** 163

slavery and, *A:* 6, 8 (ill.),
18
West Point Military Acade-
my
B: 34, 77
West Virginia
A: 34
PS: 14, 17
Western America explo-
ration
B: 106–11, 109 (ill.), 111
(ill.)
Wharton, Vernon L.
PS: 130
"What Is Religion?" (Howe)
B: 131
Wheeler, George
B: 108
Wheeling and Belmont
Bridge Company vs.
State of Pennsylvania
B: 169
Whig Party
A: 148
B: 84, 91, 92, 182, 183,
192, 210
Whiskey Ring
B: 86–87
PS: 181–82
"A Whisper in the Dark"
(Alcott)
B: 7
White Brotherhood
PS: 156
White churches
A: 60, 62
White, George H.
PS: 131
White House, sports cham-
pions and
B: 225
"White League"
PS: 192 (ill.)
White Liners
A: 159, 177–78, 184
White Southerners
African American suffrage
and, *A:* 137, 140; *PS:*
105, 135, 166
African Americans in poli-
tics and government, *A:*
150–51; *PS:* 105–6, 123,
124–25, 134, 135, 137

amnesty for, *A:* 80
Bullock, Rufus B., and, *PS:*
146
carpetbaggers and, *PS:*
144–45, 147
Civil Rights Bill of 1875
and, *PS:* 191
emancipation and, *A:*
32–33, 54–56
First Reconstruction Act
of 1867 and, *PS:* 101
free labor system and, *A:*
68
Freedmen's Bureau and,
A: 108; *PS:* 40–41
Hayes, Rutherford B., and,
PS: 198
humiliation of, *PS:* 61,
134, 137
Johnson, Andrew, and, *A:*
105; *PS:* 109, 113
Ku Klux Klan and, *PS:* 154
Lincoln, Abraham, and,
A: 7
mistreatment of African
Americans by, *A:* 129,
140
multiracial governments
and, *A:* 133, 147
new African American be-
havior and, *A:* 58–59
new social order, *PS:* 3,
4–5
plantation aristocracy
and, *A:* 86–87
rebuilding without slaves,
PS: 4–5, 58, 61
Reconstruction Acts and,
A: 146
Reconstruction era and,
A: 9
Reconstruction era taxes
and, *PS:* 141
resentment of, *A:* 73, 74;
PS: 7–8, 124–25, 141,
191
resistance to change, *A:*
89, 158–60
in South Carolina legislature, *PS:* 135–36
Union League and, *PS:* 127
White supremacists
A: 181 (ill.)

African American officials
and, *PS:* 130, 135
elections of 1868 and, *A:*
137
intimidation by, *PS:* 131
Ku Klux Klan as, *A:* 159
Reconstruction evaluation
by, *A:* 207–8
Redemption movement
and, *A:* 167–87
violence from, *PS:* 155–56
White terrorists
A: 5, 158–60
African American voters
and, *A:* 140
black churches and, *A:* 63
Enforcement Acts and, *A:*
139, 160–62
Whitman, Walt
B: 67
Whitney, Mary Watson
B: 163
Whittier, John Greenleaf
B: 71
Wilderness Campaign
B: 80
Williams, Andrew
B: 99
Williams, Thomas
B: 142 (ill.)
Will's Wonder-Book (Alcott)
B: 7
Wilson, Henry
A: 104
B: 83, 158
PS: 181
Wilson, James F.
B: 142 (ill.)
Winchester, Jonas
B: 90
Wirt, William
B: 182
Wisconsin, African Ameri-
can suffrage in
PS: 89, 166
Wise, Henry A.
B: 56
Woman's International
Peace Association
B: 130
Woman's Journal
B: 7, 129

Women
  abolitionism and, *PS:*
    94–95
  clothing of, *PS:* 8
  new roles for, *PS:* 60–61
  education and, *B:* 163,
    164, 166
Women's Education Associa-
  tion
  B: 163, 164
Women's Educational and
  Industrial Union
  B: 166
Women's National Loyal
  League
  B: 11
Women's rights
  A: 112–13
  abolitionism and, *PS:*
    94–95
  Anthony, Susan B., *B:*
    9–16, 14 (ill.)
  Douglass, Frederick, and,
    PS: 55
  Howe, Julia Ward, and, *B:*
    124, 129–30
  Stanton, Elizabeth Cady,
    B: 12–13, 14 (ill.)
Women's Rights Conven-
  tion
  B: 11, 12, 56
Women's State Temperance
  Society
  B: 11
Women's suffrage
  A: 113, 114, 114 (ill.)
  abolitionism and, *PS:* 95
  Alcott, Louisa May, and,
    B: 7
  Anthony, Susan B., and,
    B: 9, 11–16

Douglass, Frederick, and,
  PS: 55
Fifteenth Amendment
  and, *B:* 15; *PS:* 171
Fourteenth Amendment
  and, *PS:* 95–96
Howe, Julia Ward, and, *B:*
  124, 129–30, 131
Stanton, Elizabeth Cady,
  and, *B:* 12–13
Wood engraving
  B: 70
Wood, Robert H.
  A: 151–52
Woodhull, Victoria
  A: 114 (ill.)
Woodward, John Douglas
  B: 74
Words for the Hour (Howe)
  B: 127
World Parliament of Reli-
  gions
  B: 130–31
World War I
  A: 205
"World's Congress of
  Women in Behalf of In-
  ternational Peace"
  B: 130
The World's Own (Howe)
  B: 127
Wounded Knee Massacre
  B: 151
Wright, George
  B: 223
Wright, Harry
  B: 218 (ill.), **218–25**, 222
  (ill.), 224 (ill.)
Writers
  Alcott, Louisa May, *B:* 1–8
  Douglass, Frederick, *B:*
    52–61

Harte, Bret, *B:* 98–104
Howe, Julia Ward, *B:*
  124–32
The Writing Master (Eakins)
  B: 63
Wyoming, women voting in
  B: 15

Y

Yale University
  B: 24
Yankton dialect
  B: 147
Yates, Richard
  B: 78
Yellowstone National Park
  B: 105, 109, 110
Yellowstone territory
  B: 108–11, 109 (ill.)
Yulee, David
  PS: 69

Z

Zion School for Colored
  Children
  PS: 54 (ill.)
  African Americans and, *A:*
    62–63, 195
  disagreement over, *A:*
    37–38
  Douglass, Frederick, and,
    A: 23
  Radical Republicans and,
    A: 134, 170
  in Redemption era South,
    A: 196